BY THE WATERS OF BABYLON

BY THE WATERS OF BABYLON

An introduction to the History and Theology of the Exile

JAMES D. NEWSOME, Jr.

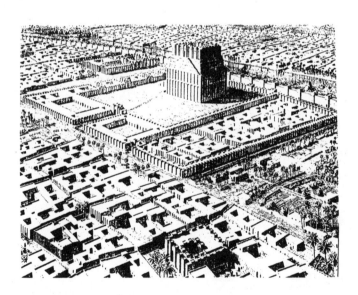

John Knox Press
ATLANTA

Illustrations in this volume are from the following sources:

Figure 20 from Georges Perrot and Charles Chipiez, *A History of Art in Chaldaea and Assyria*, trans. Walter Armstrong (London: Chapman and Hall, 1884), Vol. II.

Figures 1, 29, 32, 35, 36, 38 from Perrot and Chipiez, *History of Art in Persia* (London: Chapman and Hall, 1892).

Figures 9, 37, 39 from Perrot and Chipiez, *History of Art in Sardinia, Judaea, Syria, and Asia Minor*, trans. I. Gonino (London: Chapman and Hall, 1890), Vol. I.

Figure 16 from Perrot and Chipiez, *A History of Art in Ancient Egypt*, trans. Walter Armstrong (London: Chapman and Hall, 1883), Vol. I.

Figure 3 from Robert Koldeway, *Das Wieder Erstehende Babylon* (Liepzig: J. C. Hinrichs, 1913).

Figures 2, 7, 12, 23, 30 from Leonard W. King, *A History of Babylon* (London: Chatto & Windus, 1915).

Figures 21, 22, 25, 26 from Oscar Reuther, *Die Innenstadt von Babylon* (Leipzig: J. C. Hinrichs, 1926).

Figure 34 from Emil Herzfeld and Friederich Saare, *Iranische Felsreliefs* (Berlin: E. Wasmuth, 1910).

Figures 4, 5, 6, 8, 10, 11, 13, 14, 15, 17, 18, 19, 24, 27, 28, 31, 33 from Joseph Bonomi, *Nineveh and Its Palaces* (London: Ingram, Cooke & Co., 1853).

The Scripture quotations in this publication are from the Revised Standard Version Bible, copyright 1946, 1952, and © 1971 by the Division of Christian Education, National Council of the Churches of Christ in the U.S.A. and used by permission.

Library of Congress Cataloging in Publication Data

Newsome, James D., 1931–
    By the waters of Babylon.

    Bibliography: p.
    Includes index.
    1. Jews—History—Babylonian Captivity, 598–515 B.C. 2. Jews—History—953–586 B.C. 3. Judaism—History—To 140 B.C. 4. Bible. O. T.—History of Biblical events. I. Title.
DS121.65.N48   933   78-52441
ISBN 0-8042-0016-5

For Sis, Laura, Carolyn,
Dick, and Burns

My thoughts and feelings seem to be getting more and more like those of the Old Testament, and in recent months I have been reading the Old Testament much more than the New. It is only when one knows the unutterability of the name of God that one can utter the name of Jesus Christ; it is only when one loves life and the earth so much that without them everything seems to be over that one can believe in the resurrection and a new world; it is only when one submits to God's law that one can speak of grace; and it is only when God's wrath and vengeance are hanging as grim realities over the heads of one's enemies that something of what it means to love and forgive them can touch our hearts.

Dietrich Bonhoeffer
Letter from Prison
Second Sunday in Advent,
1943*

*Eberhard Bethge, ed., *Letters and Papers from Prison* (New York: MacMillan Co., 1953, rev. ed. 1967), p. 103.

Preface

Every human story of any significance at all is a tale of hope and despair. In our schemes of categorization, those tales in which hope predominates are termed "comedies," while those in which the despair is master are "tragedies." The two theatrical masks, one smiling, the other frowning, which are represented in some form in nearly every playhouse in the world, are an attempt to symbolize the dark and the light of life.

The story which this book undertakes to tell is, on the face of it, a narrative of calamity, a tale of physical suffering and of spiritual disillusion. And so it should, from one vantage point at least, be labeled a tragedy and shelved alongside the *Antigones* and the *Macbeths* in the library of the human heart.

Yet one consideration prevents such a cataloging, one lyric echo in the midst of the brutal noises. It is the faith of the people who are caught up in the mélange of cracked hearts and broken bodies. It is their conviction that the God whom they worship will somehow impose a meaning upon all the violent events, or that, if that meaning is already there, he will lead them to understand it. And it is their further faith that, when that meaning is discovered, it will be a quality of compassion and grace which are present only because he has placed them there.

To some this tale will appear a supreme example of man's ability to delude himself, a case study in his penchant for whistling through the graveyard of his buried hopes. For others, who have seen far more flagrant cruelty and desolation than this story entails, the hope which survived the great disasters at the end of the Old Testament period will seem all too easy and trivial.

But in between, there are many who have been touched by the events related in this volume and who have taken with greatest seriousness both the tragedy and the hope. And they will have found in the faith in God which spawned that hope—a faith sometimes flickering, sometimes misplaced, sometimes sterilely institutionalized, but also frequently courageous and vital—a key to the unlocking of all human confrontations with tragedy. They will find a prelude to the ultimate expression of human hope, the Easter faith in the Risen Christ.

This volume attempts to tell the story of the Jewish people during those years before the destruction of Jerusalem in 587 B.C., to profile the Jewish experience under Babylonian rule, and to sketch the shape of those hopes which led to Jerusalem's restoration under the Davidic princes Sheshbazzar and Zerubbabel.

The tale is told in the first instance because, in spite of the fact that it constitutes a kind of climax to the Old Testament narrative and in spite of the fact that it witnesses the laying of the foundations of both modern Judaism and Christianity, the period in question is one of the least understood of Old Testament history. Part of the reason for this lack of understanding is that so few historical records survived this era, far fewer than have come down to us from certain earlier periods in Israel's past. Yet important parts of the puzzle have fallen into place in recent years, rendering our ignorance of the times less extensive than before.

Also, this story is told because it has rarely been told before, except in such a manner as either to gloss over important details or so as to appeal only to specialists in biblical literature and history. This volume is offered in the hope that a portrait of the times may be drawn in such a manner as is true to the many nuances of feeling and action which characterized those unsettled but creative years, yet in such a way that the reader is not mired down in the slough of excessive detail.

Finally and most importantly, the book is written in the hope that the faith which sustained the people of God—a faith which was ultimately realized in a manner far transcending even their own visions of man's future with God—will strike a responsive chord in the reader, who must also wrestle, whoever he is, with his own defeats and hopes for restoration.

No effort has been made on these pages to instruct the scholar, who will find here a deep indebtedness to several generations of pioneers in biblical research. Rather this volume is intended for the serious student of the Bible who is not a specialist, but who is interested in inquiring into the history and spiritual experience of those people who are responsible for writing a large slice of the Old Testament and whose struggles of faith are in many ways parallel to those of our own times. The reader should be alerted to the fact that the author's imagination has been used to fill in certain small chinks in the story for which no solid evidence exists, much as an archaeologist might restore broken bits of ancient pottery by joining them with mortar of his own mixing. Into this category would fall the description of the *coup d'etat* against Amel-Marduk, the reflections of the Jewish farmer upon witnessing the return of the entourage of Prince Sheshbazzar, and other, less important, details. The purpose, of course, is not to blur the distinction between fiction and fact, but to present the exile within a context of its dramatic and narrative unity.

The reader who wishes to probe more deeply into certain of the events and personalities with which this book deals will find in the footnotes and bibliography suggestions for ample further exploration. Wherever possible, books and articles have been mentioned which are likely to be available in the well-stocked library of the local clergyman or in that of the local parish church.

Non-Jewish names of the Old Testament period are frequently troublesome because their biblical spellings are often different from their forms in other ancient languages. Generally, "native" spellings have been used (Nebuchadrezzar instead of the biblical Nebuchadnezzar, Amel-Marduk for Evil-Merodach, etc.), although in the case of the final Babylonian emperor, Nabonidus (the form used by the ancient Greek historians) seemed more satisfactory than the Babylonian Nabu-na'id.

Modern scholarship has necessarily filled a vacuum by applying names of its own manufacture to certain of the anonymous biblical authors of the seventh and sixth centuries B.C. and to some of the literature produced during those years. For the most part these names have been used here (e.g., the Chronicler, Priestly History), but in two instances modern scholarly labels have been passed over in favor of other phrases which seemed either more natural (Babylonian Isaiah for Deutero or Second Isaiah) or less likely to incur the charge of anachronism (Great History for Deuteronomic History). But in both cases the reader will understand that no difference in meaning is implied.

Finally, I wish to express my deep gratitude to the Session and congregation of the First Presbyterian Church of Paducah, Kentucky, who generously granted to me, then their pastor, a study leave of one year, during which time this book was written.

James D. Newsome, Jr.
Epiphany 1978

Contents

I.

NEBUCHADREZZAR

(605–562 B.C.)

Look among the nations, and see;
wonder and be astounded.
For I am doing a work in your days
that you would not believe if told.
For lo, I am rousing the Chaldeans,
that bitter and hasty nation,
who march through the breadth of the earth,
to seize habitations not their own.
Dread and terrible are they;
their justice and dignity proceed from themselves.
Their horses are swifter than leopards,
more fierce than the evening wolves;
their horsemen press proudly on.
Yea, their horsemen come from afar;
they fly like an eagle swift to devour.
They all come for violence;
terror of them goes before them.
They gather captives like sand.
At kings they scoff,
and of rulers they make sport.
They laugh at every fortress,
for they heap up earth and take it.
Then they sweep by like the wind and go on,
guilty men, whose own might is their god!

—Habakkuk 1:5–11

Chapter One

The swift cannot flee away,
nor the warrior escape;
in the north by the river Euphrates
they have stumbled and fallen.

—Jeremiah 46:6

Seventeen hundred miles of contorted, vein-like wanderings have earned for the Euphrates the distinction of being the longest river in western Asia. It begins as simple runoff from the melted snows of the mountains of Armenia and, after a slow descent of nearly 12,000 feet, finally disgorges itself into the warm brine of the Persian Gulf. To the ancient Egyptians it was "the river which flows backwards," that is, in the direction opposite to the Nile. But to the Babylonians, whose home straddled its banks, it was simply "the great river." Both Egyptians and Babylonians had reason to commemorate the Euphrates, for this stream was to wash away the blood of their two powerful armies which, in mortal combat, wrote a crimson chapter in the history of the ancient Near East. It was a bellicose collision which, although few realized it at the time, sounded the death knell of the royal City of David.

To Carchemish beside the Euphrates the Egyptian Pharaoh Neco II had dispatched a large contingent of his army, several thousand strong, in the effort to plunder what remained of the moribund Assyrian Empire. The very mention of Assyria had once sent convulsions of terror down the spines of peoples from the Nile to the Tigris to Lake Van. But Assyria had now fallen victim to her own cruelty and shortsightedness and, beset by rebellion within and by invasion from without, was now a corpse awaiting burial. In a final lunge for life, the Assyrian monarch, Asshur-uballit, had called for help from Egypt, and the Egyptians responded, not out of love for Assyria, but in the hope of seizing for themselves a slice of the estate Assyria was soon to leave involuntarily to her neighbors.

Assyria's nemeses, and thus the foes whom the Egyptians had challenged in coming to Assyria's aid, were the Medes and the Babylonians. The Medes were a group of tough, self-willed people who lived in the highlands to the east of Mesopotamia and thus just beyond the limit of Assyrian authority. Their success in resisting Assyrian incursions over the years was probably due to a combination of personal fortitude and a land well fitted by nature for defense. Now in the final quarter of the seventh

Figure 1. Assyrian Standard. Monument from Nineveh.

century the Medes, witnessing the growing fatigue of Assyria, had turned predator and had begun to probe for the Assyrian jugular.

The Babylonians, on the other hand, were, like scores of other luckless peoples, subjects of the Assyrians. In 689 B.C. Assyrian armies under Sennacherib had entered Babylon, where a mighty kingdom had flourished a millenium before, had subjected the people to the Assyrian will, and laid waste the city amid great loss of Babylonian life. But the Babylonians ultimately became alert to the same internal Assyrian rot which had encouraged the Medes, and in 626 a Babylonian prince, Nabopolassar, raised an army of his compatriots and fell upon the oppressors of his city. The Assyrians grudgingly withdrew and, after a decade and a half of sporadic fighting, a combined force of Medes and Babylonians, joined by a fierce northern group, the Scythians, assaulted the Assyrian capital of Ninevah. They destroyed the defending army and much of the city's population, murdered the king, and set about dividing the spoils among themselves.

Many miles away, the Hebrew prophet Nahum captured the emotions of the moment:

> Ninevah is like a pool
>   whose waters run away.
> "Halt! Halt!" they cry;
>   but none turns back.

> Plunder the silver,
>   plunder the gold!
> There is no end of treasure,
>   or wealth of every precious thing.
>   (Nah. 2:8f.)

A tiny fragment of the Assyrian military survived and fled to the west in the hope of salvaging its frayed fortunes. It was ignored, for the moment, by the victorious Medes and Babylonians who demonstrated unusual moderation in that, instead of fighting between themselves for the captured booty, they halved the Assyrian carcass. To the Medes went a crescent shaped swatch of territory running from north to east around the perimeter of the Tigris-Euphrates watershed, while the Babylonians laid claim to the Mesopotamian valley proper and to the lands westward toward the Mediterranean Sea. With the border between themselves thus peacefully secured, the Medes and the Babylonians were at liberty to focus their energies in other directions, the Medes to the north and east, the Babylonians to the west and south, in the hope of further conquests.

It was this arrangement which brought the Babylonians into hostile confrontation with the Egyptians. The latter had long cast greedy eyes upon the rich margin of the eastern Mediterranean, where Egypt had

Figure 2. The Assyrian Army in Chaldea. From an Assyrian Relief.

brandished her sovereignty many years before. During the long years of
the Assyrian rule over the area, Egyptian armies rarely ventured outside
the protective shell of their own homeland, and even less frequently did
they cherish hopes of dominating Palestine and Syria. Yet Damascus,
Tyre, and Jerusalem offered fat opportunities, if only they could be
seized. Thus, the fall of Ninevah presented to Egypt the chance to attempt
that which it previously dared not do. The plea for help from the shredded
Assyrian remnant, now encamped at Haran, was an unneeded pretext to
send a massive Egyptian force across the Sinai and into the Palestinian
heartland. But by now the Babylonians were moving west and south to
consolidate a grip upon their new positions, and collision was inevitable.

The first shock of arms occurred in and around the spot where the
fleeing Assyrians had taken refuge. Haran, an important oasis which
Hebrew tradition associated with the migration of Abraham (Gen. 11:31),
is some two hundred miles west of Ninevah in the upper reaches of the
Euphrates drainage, and in that direction the Babylonian military machine set itself following the sack of Ninevah. There was some delay caused
by the necessity to regroup and resupply themselves. And there was also
the matter of tribute monies to be collected from the newly subjected
peoples along the way. Thus by the time the Babylonians arrived in the
neighborhood of Haran, a sizable Egyptian force awaited them. The duel
which followed was to last for more than half a decade, a bloodbath for
which the prize was to be control of that fruitful land from the Sinai
Desert to the border of modern Turkey. Carchemish was the climactic
result.

That there ultimately was a result at all may be credited to a new personality who in 605 B.C. emerged as a crafty and vigorous sculptor of human events, the Babylonian crown prince, Nebuchadrezzar.[1] Twenty one years had passed since Nabopolassar first raised the standard of revolt in a Babylon which languished under the heel of the Assyrian overlord, twenty one years of intermittent struggle during which the tyrants had been butchered and the glories of the Old Babylon of a thousand years before, the Babylon of the legendary King Hammurabi, had been recalled. But now Nabopolassar was aged and sick and soon to die. And so to Nebuchadrezzar the failing king entrusted the command of Babylon's war machine, and the prince, revealing that first dash of genius and energy which was eventually to mark him as one of the premier leaders in world history, rushed to the west and quickly marched his troops toward the important Egyptian garrison at Carchemish.

The other young warlord had also been on the move. Leaving his capital at Memphis some weeks before, Neco[2] had led a strong column of infantry and horse northward through Palestine and into Syria in the obvious effort to locate the main Babylonian force and, in the process, to claim as much precious territory as possible. Yet the Egyptians were too late. Even as the Pharaoh urged his men and equipment northward, Nebuchadrezzar, with an enormous Babylonian force at his back, easily forded the Euphrates a few miles downstream from Carchemish and, moving quickly up the west bank of the river, fell suddenly and viciously upon the Egyptian garrison there.

There was carnage all around, but the outcome was never in doubt. Babylonian swordsmen butchered the flower of Egyptian soldiery, while Nebuchadrezzar's horsemen quickly ran down and impaled the survivors who tried to escape. The Babylonian Chronicle, a contemporary history written upon tablets of baked clay and whose tone is unfailingly sober and terse, says simply but forcefully of Carchemish: "Nebuchadrezzar accomplished the Egyptians' defeat and beat them into non-existence." The blunt, brutal meaning of Carchemish was that all of Syria and Palestine were to be added to the Babylonian conquests. Not immediately

Figure 3. A Cuneiform Inscription of Nebuchadrezzar.

and not compliantly on the part of the Egyptians or of the people of the region, but ultimately and forceably all of the lands from Mesopotamia to the Mediterranean would lie under Babylonian sovereignty. Even the Egyptian homeland itself would be imperiled.

Hardly had the corpses of Carchemish been interred than word reached Nebuchadrezzar that his father, the old King Nabopolassar, had died. The prince hurried to Babylon where, on the first day of the Babylonian month Elul (September 6) in the year 605 B.C., he was crowned king. We have been left no record of the festivities surrounding the coronation, but it takes little imagination to visualize the splendor which must have accompanied, first, the ostentatious funeral of the imperious Nabopolassar, and then the florid rites of enthronement for his son. Elaborate prayers to Marduk, dancing in the streets, freely flowing wine, all were surely abundant.

Figure 4. Servants to the Assyrian King's Table.

But Nebuchadrezzar was not one to dally over wine, or over prayer, for that matter. With the echoes of the celebrations still reverberating within the enclosure of the city walls, the new king rode out through the great Ishtar Gate and, with the morning sun at his back, began his return to the theater of war. It is probable that during these months Damascus, Tyre, Sidon, Jerusalem, and other cities were visited by Nebuchadrezzar or by his lieutenants, and peacefully, but not happily, they swore allegiance to this fresh master from beside the Euphrates and emptied their chests into his own.

But there were a few who demurred. Ashkelon was one, an ancient Philistine city due west of Jerusalem on the Mediterranean coast. Ashkelon had, like her neighbors, formerly been a victim of Assyrian soldiers and tax collectors, and now that Assyria was dead, she had no intention of submitting herself to a new Mesopotamian master, especially with still powerful Egypt so near. So the city refused Nebuchadrezzar, whereupon the engines of siege were drawn up by the Babylonians and the town was assaulted.

By coincidence a pathetic product of this siege has come down to us— a small piece of papyrus upon which, in a bold yet graceful Aramaic script, the king of Ashkelon appealed to Pharaoh Neco for help as the Babylonian soldiers bore down on his city. It was discovered a few years ago at Saqqarah, in Egypt, and in spite of some deterioration, it may be read as follows:

> To Lord of Kingdoms, Pharaoh, thy servant Adon, King of Ashkelon. May Ashtarte, mistress of heaven and earth, and Baalshemiam, the great god, make the throne of the Lord of the Kingdoms, Pharaoh, enduring as the days of heaven. That I have written to my Lord is to inform thee that the troops of the king of Babylon have advanced as far as Aphek and have begun to . . . they have taken . . . and . . . For the Lord of Kingdoms, Pharaoh, knows that thy servant cannot stand alone against the king of Babylon. May it therefore please him not to forsake me. For thy servant is loyal to my Lord and thy servant remembers his kindness as this region is my Lord's possession. But if the king of Babylon takes it, he will set up a governor in the land, and . . .[3]

The appeal was in vain. Ashkelon's walls were breached, the city plundered, and many of the citizens put to the sword. Then poor King Adon was dispatched into captivity in Babylon, as were a number of his noblemen, soldiers, and skilled workmen. A surviving Babylonian document dating from a number of years later shows that many of them were then still there.

Nebuchadrezzar was now lord of that entire slice of geography extending from the Sinai Desert to the foothills of Armenia, and he ruled as well over most of the Mesopotamian valley, the old heartland of the defunct Assyrian Empire. The revenues from these possessions were considerable, and by means of them Nebuchadrezzar provisioned his army and honed the edges of its fighting skills. He also applied these monies to the improvement of social services in Babylon itself and to projects intended to beautify the city. Nebuchadrezzar had read well the histories of the Assyrian kings, and the lesson was not lost upon him that prosperity and contentment at home were essential to a despot's firm grip upon his scepter of state.

Pharaoh Neco, meanwhile, had been licking his wounds. The destruction of Egyptian military power at Carchemish had been extensive and painful, a fact made evident not simply by Neco's deaf ear to the plea from King Adon of Ashkelon, but even more by the total submission of all southern Palestine to Babylon. But by 601 the Pharaoh had crossed his borders and turned northward with a large body of foot soldiers, supported by a liberal contingent of chariots and horses. For more than three years Neco had been a virtual prisoner in his own kingdom, and his willingness to challenge Nebuchadrezzar now implies that those years had been devoted largely to designs for revenge. The Babylonian Chronicle suggests that the Egyptian sortie was the result of a thrust by Nebuchadrezzar toward the Egyptian homeland, and such may well have been the case. But the outcome of the duel of arms suggests that a great deal of careful planning had gone into the Egyptian preparations.

As no Egyptian account of the battle has come to light, we are dependent upon our single Babylonian source, the Chronicle, brief and sketchy though it is. Without naming the site of the combat, the Babylonian historians report tersely:

> In open battle they [i.e., Nebuchadrezzar and Neco] smote the breasts of each other and inflicted great havoc upon each other. The king of Babylon and his troops turned back and returned to Babylon.[4]

The battle of 601 was, at best, a draw, although more probably an Egyptian victory may be read from the account, as the Babylonian Chronicle goes on to log the fact that, contrary to his usual custom, Nebuchadrezzar spent the entire next year at home, resupplying his army with chariots and horses. Such a statement may also indicate that it was an Egyptian superiority in these weapons which turned the tide in their favor. Although information concerning the station where the clash of arms occurred has not survived, we may believe that it took place somewhere in southern Palestine, the area of maximum Babylonian exposure to Egypt. And its consequence was an outbreak of rebellion among some of those who lived in the area, a rebellion partly motivated by a longing to be free of the hated Babylonians, but also by the anticipation that Neco's authority was about to be imposed in place of Nebuchadrezzar. One such revolt took place in Jerusalem at this time led by King Jehoiakim.

Our information concerning the events of the next few months is scanty, but we may visualize a chastened, but still proud Nebuchadrezzar at home nursing his wounds. Not until two years after the clash with Neco do we find him again with his army in the field. But in this instance the field of operations is in the north, far from the reaches of the Pharaoh. Here Nebuchadrezzar's activity consists largely of showing his standards in order to assist his revenue agents and of a few punative raids against desert nomads.

Figure 5. The Assyrian King Hunting Lion.

Meanwhile Neco seems to have made some effort to reimpose himself upon the area of southern Palestine. A notice in the Book of Jeremiah indicates the presence of Egyptian arms in Gaza perhaps after Neco's encounter with Nebuchadrezzar (Jer. 47:1). And Jehoiakim's defiance of Babylon may have been sparked by an Egyptian military presence in the vicinity of Jerusalem or by the influence of Egyptian agents at the Judean court. Yet Neco, in spite of these and other possible efforts, was unable to gain a permanent foothold in the south of Palestine.

The reason was simply the fierce energy and determination of Nebuchadrezzar. In 598 the Babylonian king descended upon rebellious Jerusalem, the most important stronghold lost as a result of the bloodletting of 601, and in the early months of the following year humiliated the city and its new eighteen-year-old king, Jehoiachin. The biblical side of this tragedy will be told presently, but notice should here be made of this entry in the Babylonian Chronicle:

> In the seventh year, the month of Kislev [December], the king of Babylon mustered his troops, marched to Palestine, and besieged the City of Judah and on the second day of the month of Adar [February], he siezed the city and captured the king. He appointed there a king of his own choice, received its heavy tribute and sent it to Babylon.[5]

To this information may be appended a brief statement of the Second Book of Kings.

> And the king of Egypt did not come again out of his land, for the king of Babylon had taken all that belonged to the king of Egypt from the Brook of Egypt to the river Euphrates.
>
> (2 Kings 24:7)

Southern Palestine, therefore, was now firmly in Babylonian hands and would remain so for most of what was left of Nebuchadrezzar's lifetime.

For his part, Neco seems not to have challenged the outcome at Jerusalem and, indeed, appears not to have engaged the Babylonians in combat again in the few years of life remaining to him.

The Babylonian Chronicle reveals that at this time Nebuchadrezzar settled into a relatively uneventful period in his life. The following year was the occasion of a journey by the monarch into the north of the kingdom, near the site of his great victory at Carchemish. No reason for the expedition is given, but uncharacteristically, the Chronicle fails to mention the presence of the army, quite possibly implying that the upper reaches of the Euphrates watershed were sufficiently secure to enable the king to travel about with only minimal protection.

The final months of the year did witness trouble of some kind in the east, as Nebuchadrezzar is to be found at the head of a column of troops in a sweep through the Tigris basin in search of some unnamed intruders. And a rebellion at home in 595 resulted in a number of deaths before the ringleaders, whose identity we may shortly discover, were captured and brought to a cruel justice. But these appear to have been but ripples upon the surface of a Babylon whose position in world affairs was now secure under the leadership of a vigorous and resourceful ruler. The empire embraced hundreds of thousands of square miles of land, much of it fruitful and abundant, rich in minerals and other natural resources. It was, furthermore, a land populated by peoples representing a wide variety of ethnic stocks and possessing a large capacity for productive labor. Economic wealth and military power thus became the stout pillars upon which Nebuchadrezzar's Babylon rested, and they proved to be a secure foundation for the duration of the monarch's days.

At this juncture the Babylonian Chronicle, our chief source of information concerning the place of Nebuchadrezzar in Babylonian history, breaks off. It is not unreasonable to assume that the Chronicle recorded the major events for each year of Nebuchadrezzar's reign, for there is an existing tablet dealing with the activity of one of his successors, Nergal-shar-usur, during the years 557–556. But until further tablets relating to the rule of Nebuchadrezzar come to light, we must rely upon non-Babylonian sources for information pertaining to his activities after 594.

The Old Testament, for example, reports a second rebellion in Jerusalem, this one led by Nebuchadrezzar's own puppet upon the Judean throne, Zedekiah, an insurrection which was crushed in 587 with vicious finality. In addition, the Jewish historian Josephus records an uprising on the part of Tyre, one of the richest of the cities subject to Babylonian rule, which dragged on for thirteen years until finally suppressed in 572. And there is also a fragmentary Babylonian account of hostilities between Nebuchadrezzar and Pharaoh Amasis in 567.

But through these and possibly other threats to his sovereignty Nebuchadrezzar moved with resolution and skill. Cities were destroyed, entire populations crushed, and an innumerable quantity of human beings
subjected to the most terrible suffering in the pursuit of the single goal
of securing the imperial authority. Like the Assyrian kings before him,
Nebuchadrezzar combined sagacity and ruthlessness in the effort to milk
the greatest possible treasure from his subject peoples. Most of those who
resisted received a single short, sharp reply: the sword. Others were spared
the sword only to be paraded off into permanent exile in some distant
stretch of the empire or in Babylon itself. The stone tablets unearthed
by the archaeologist's spade a few years ago, which name the captives
from Ashkelon, also mention as involuntary guests of Nebuchadrezzar individuals from Tyre, Byblos, Arvad, Egypt, Persia, Lydia, and Greece.

To his determination as an overlord must be added Nebuchadrezzar's
brilliance as a military and political tactician. We can glean few details
of his battle strategies from the laconic cadences of the Babylonian
Chronicle, but the account of Carchemish leaves the reader room to en-
vision a swift, forced march of the Babylonian troops, a furtive crossing
of the Euphrates, possibly at night, and a surprise assault upon an astonished Egyptian garrison. Beyond that, the duration and tenacity of his
sieges of Jerusalem and Tyre reveal that a dogged patience was one of
Nebuchadrezzar's military virtues. And his cleverly arranged marriage to
the daughter of the Medean king resulted, during his lifetime, in har-
monious relations with Babylon's collaborators
in the conquest of Assyria.

But if Nebuchadrezzar could be brutal as a
master and cunning as a soldier and diplomat,
to his compatriots he was the soul of beneficence,
if, that is, one may venture a judgment on the
basis of his program of public works in Babylon
itself. In the Book of Daniel, the king, standing
on the roof of his royal palace and surveying
the sprawling city below, asks, "Is this not great
Babylon, which I have built by my mighty
power as the royal residence and for the glory
of my majesty" (Dan. 4:30)? It is a rhetorical
question, for all the ancient world knew that
by the sheer force of Nebuchadrezzar's will and
genius a new Babylon had emerged from the
rubble left by the plundering Assyrians a half
century before.

Many of Nebuchadrezzar's architectural accomplishments were of a military nature, such

Figure 6.
Assyrian Priest with
Sacrificial Gazelle.

as an enormous outer wall, protecting an existing smaller one, which encircled Babylon and, bristling with towers and turrets, made the city all but impregnable to hostile military action. It is a tribute to the skill of Nebuchadrezzar, the buider, that when Babylon fell to the invader less than a century later, it was not by defeat of arms but by resignation of the spirit.

Temples and houses of worship were refurbished and adorned. The Greek historian Herodotus claims that the ziggurat in Babylon, a mini-mountain of stone and brick supporting a religious shrine on its summit (probably the Tower of Babel referred to in Genesis 11), was enhanced by Nebuchadrezzar to more splendid proportions. The house of Babylon's chief god, Marduk, was likewise renovated and the worship of that deity given a fresh impetus. In the neighboring towns of Borsippa, Larsa, Uruk, Ur, and Dilbat, old temples were renovated or new ones constructed. And even the streets were paved for spiritual purposes, as the following inscription, discovered a number of years ago in the ruins of Babylon, demonstrates:

> Nebuchadrezzar, King of Babylon, son of Nabopolassar, King of Babylon, am I. Of the streets of Babylon for the procession of the great lord Marduk with slabs of limestone I built the causeway. Oh, Marduk, my lord, grant eternal life.[6]

Nebuchadrezzar invested enormous funds in a new palace for himself and his harem. This sumptuous residence presumably housed the fabled "Hanging Gardens," cascading tiers of greenery which the king installed to compensate his Median queen, Amuhia, for the loss of her verdant upland home and which the ancient Greeks would count among the Seven Wonders of the World. The great Ishtar Gate, a splendid portal in the northern wall of the city through which one passed from the grand Processional Way into the flat countryside beyond, was extensively reworked by Nebuchadrezzar. And one account even credits the monarch with the digging of a new canal from Babylon to the Persian Gulf, a distance of several hundred miles.

These accomplishments were impressive not only by virtue of their size and cost, but also because of their artistry. Excavations earlier in this century at the Ishtar Gate revealed massive towers whose surfaces of glazed and brightly colored bricks were ornamented with majestic bas-relief lions and richly colored flowers and plants. Coming upon this Babylon, which rode as a bright ship upon the dull brown ocean of the Mesopotamian plain, the traveler must have been struck as by a veritable El Dorado.

Nebuchadrezzar's impact upon Babylon, however, was not entirely architectural. Under the impetus of his energetic spirit, a renaissance was

Figure 7. Bas-Relief Lion from Babylon.

kindled in law, literature, and religion which, for a time at least, promised to make the New Babylonian Empire as dynamic a force as had been
the Old Babylon of a thousand years before. It was, in fact, the avowed
purpose of Nebuchadrezzar and his generation to recapture the soul of
the Old Babylon and to make it their own. This was the Babylon which
had scaled lofty pinnacles in letters and in arts, the Babylon of King
Hamurabbi in whose name the codification of law taught lasting lessons
in jurisprudence and laid down important rules for the conduct of business and commerce. Not realizing that they were of a different ethnic
stock, the New Babylonians mistakenly honored the Old as their ancestors, and they imitated them in their acts of worship, in their writing
of literature, and in their courts of law.

In many respects, this renaissance of Babylonian ways was superficial
and thin. The New Babylonian spirit, in spite of the older, more elevated
influences, remained restricted and hollow, for the gods seemed as far
away as the stars and planets with which they were often identified. And
as for poetry and letters, these were frequently leaden and earthbound.

Yet there were certain genuine achievements. The tight links between
religious faith and astrology in the New Babylon led to a close scrutiny
of the heavens and produced an extremely accurate record of eclipses of
sun and moon, the movements of the planets, and other celestial phe-
nomena. It also seems to have been the New Babylonians who came upon
the concept of the seven day week, and who first divided a day into twelve
double hours of 120 minutes each (which is probably the reason the faces
of our clocks are marked into twelve hourly gradations). And as for
poetry, the New Babylonian renaissance, in spite of its wanness, was
capable of the following intercession in Nebuchadrezzar's name to the
great god Marduk:

O eternal prince! Lord of all being!
As for the king whom thou lovest, and
Whose name thou hast proclaimed
As was pleasing to thee,
Do thou lead aright his life,
Guide him in a straight path.
I am the prince, obedient to thee,
The creature of thy hand;
Thou hast created me, and
With dominion over all people
Thou hast entrusted me.
According to thy grace, O Lord,
Which thou didst bestow on
All people,
Cause me to love thy supreme dominion,
And create in my heart
The worship of thy god-head,
And grant whatever is pleasing to thee,
Because thou hast fashioned my life.[7]

In 562 Nebuchadrezzar died, having ruled Babylon for 44 years. He passed on to his son, Amel-Marduk, an extensive and wealthy dominion, but one laced with restlessness and unease whose single cohesive force had been the personality of the king. That Nebuchadrezzar's successors were not his equals is betrayed by Babylon's slow spiral into oblivion.

II.

CATASTROPHE

(621–587 B.C.)

How lonely sits the city
*   that was full of people!*
How like a widow has she become,
*   she that was great among the nations!*
She that was a princess among the cities
*   has become a vassal.*

She weeps bitterly in the night,
*   tears on her cheeks;*
among all her lovers
*   she has none to comfort her;*
all her friends have dealt treacherously with her,
*   they have become her enemies.*

Judah has gone into exile because of affliction
*   and hard servitude;*
she dwells now among the nations,
*   but finds no resting place;*
her pursuers have all overtaken her
*   in the midst of her distress.*

—Lamentations 1:1–3

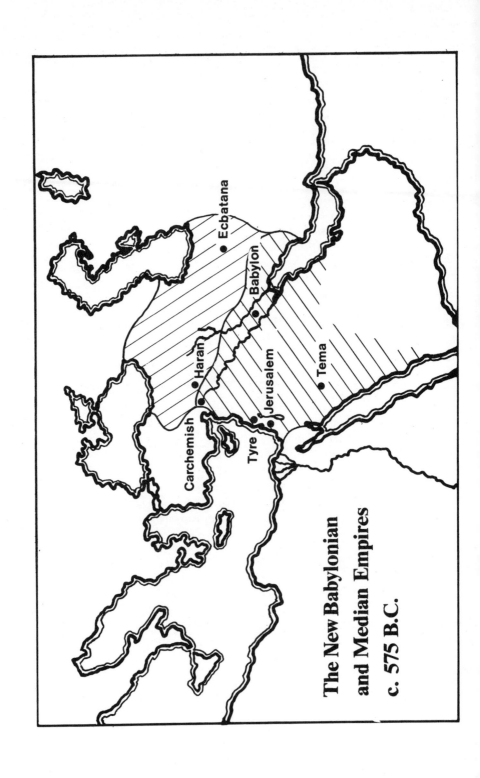

The New Babylonian
and Median Empires
c. 575 B.C.

Ecbatana

Babylon

Haran

Jerusalem

Tema

Carchemish

Tyre

Chapter Two

*These are the statutes and ordinances which you shall be
careful to do in the land which the* LORD, *the God of
your fathers, has given you to possess. . . . You shall seek
the place which the* LORD *your God will choose out of all
your tribes to put his name and make his habitation
there; thither you shall go, and thither you shall bring
your burnt offerings and your sacrifices. . . .*

—Deuteronomy 12:1, 5f.

The Reformation of King Josiah

On a day in 621 B.C., Josiah, King of Judah, received an unusual
object (2 Kings 22:3f.). A scroll containing a collection of Israel's ancient
Law, together with certain historical narratives and commentaries upon
that Law, had been discovered during repairs to the Jerusalem Temple.[8]
Although the king may not have not known it, the document possessed a
long history even before it found its way into his hands. Originally composed among scribal and priestly circles of the Northern Kingdom some-
time after its fall to the Assyrian armies of Sargon II, the scroll was a call
to spiritual arms. Looking back upon those stormy years when the Hebrew refugees under Moses struggled in the wilderness to find their own
identity before God and to prepare themselves to seize the land which
had been promised them, the document proclaimed the urgency of the
genuine worship of God and the necessity of repudiating all base and
idolatrous forms of devotion.

> And now, Israel, what does the LORD your God require of you, but to
> fear the LORD your God, to walk in all his ways, to love him, to serve the
> LORD your God with all your heart and with all your soul, and to keep
> the commandments and statutes of the LORD, which I command you this
> day for your good?
>
> (Deut. 10:12f.)

The manner in which this scroll, which men were later to call Deuteronomy, found it's way into the Temple is unknown. When the king
heard its words, however, he shredded his robes as an act of repentence
that God's people should have allowed this Law to slip into oblivion,
and soon royal messengers were fanning out over the countryside to implement the scroll's demands.

However deep the king's spiritual motives may have been in acting
in this manner, Josiah was also twisting the tail of that old tiger, Assyria.

Figure 8. A Winged Assyrian Deity.

For almost one hundred years, Jerusalem had been Assyria's bone, or to be precise, one of that cat's many bones. The meatier portions of her life having been gnawed away, Jerusalem had endured indignities to her spirit and to her purse. Mountainous payments of annual revenue into the Assyrian coffers and the introduction of the worship of Assyrian gods into the Jerusalem Temple were the ransom paid to prevent Assyrian troops from occupying the city and rendering it into a wasteland, as they had done to Jerusalem's sister, Samaria. Even when, as under King Hezekiah, Jerusalem rebelled against Assyrian domination, the beast was merely held at bay.

But now the tiger was losing its teeth. The Assyrian king Ashurbanipal had died six years before, following a reign of four decades. And it was in the subsequent year that the Babylonian Nabopolassar had raised an army to chase the Assyrians out of his homeland while, not far to the north, the Medes created mischief on their Assyrian frontier. All of that occurred hundreds of miles away, but its effect upon Judah did not go unfelt. As the Assyrian military presence upon King Josiah's borders grew slowly but unmistakably more relaxed, the king had first decreased the hated tribute monies, then left them off altogether.

When ultimately the Assyrian bowmen fell back to protect their own homeland, Josiah's soldiers moved out to claim the abandoned positions. Samaria, Megiddo, and Gilead, over which Jerusalem had once before been sovereign in the golden days of David and Solomon, were again placed under the standards of Judah's royal house. And now the newly discovered Book of the Law provided an unexpected but welcome spiritual dimension to Judah's quest for freedom.

Josiah's Reformation of 621 accomplished several important things. The pure worship of God according to the ancient rubrics was declared essential for Israel's life, and the remaining vestiges of paganism and idolatry were swept from the Temple. The Assyrian and Canaanite shrines which had flourished there were violently removed, and the Temple itself was cleansed and rededicated. The ancient festival of Passover, that victorious remembrance of God's deliverance of his people from Egyptian bondage, a celebration which had been allowed to lapse, was restored by Josiah amid popular jubilation.

The effects of the Reformation, however, were not confined to Jerusalem. There had always existed throughout the countryside large numbers of local shrines, manned by rural priests, where prayer and sacrifice were regularly offered. Since many of these spots had been places of Canaanite worship before the Hebrew conquest, it was not always clear to which god or gods a particular shrine was dedicated. The result was that many gods were often worshipped at these country altars, sometimes

one after another by their several devotees, at other times all at once in
a polytheistic amalgam. The Judean vassalage to Assyria, with its im-
portation of Assyrian gods, added further confusion and compromise to
the integrity of the rural shrines.

In the spirit of the new-found Book of the Law, Josiah suppressed
these country altars and the vivid rituals, with their frequent overtones
of magic and sexual lust, which were practiced there. No longer were
men to worship willy-nilly where and how they wished, the king main-
tained. Only in the Jerusalem Temple and only according to the liturgy
presided over by the proper priests of God could the true and authentic
worship of Israel's Deity be performed.

In addition to its attention to the liturgy of worship, the Reformation
of 621 included a fresh call to individual moral action, and it proclaimed
as an ethical ideal the belief that mercy and justice are the highest fulfillment of the Law and traditions of Israel. Honesty in the transaction
of business, compassion toward the weak and distressed, a respectful regard for the resources of the land—these and other axioms of personal
and national behavior were raised to equal standing with the proper
worship of God as a means by which Judah should respond to her special
place as a covenant people before the Lord.

> Justice, and only justice, you shall follow, that you may live and inherit
> the land which the LORD your God gives you.
>
> (Deut. 16:20)

Yet morality must be more than a matter of simple behavior and action, just as worship must be more than a matter of correct Temple
prayers and sacrifice. Judah's mandate from her God is that both her
morality and her piety be rooted in an inner attitude of confidence and
trust in the Lord.

> For this commandment which I command you this day is not too hard
> for you, neither is it far off. . . . But the word [of God] is very near you;
> it is in your mouth and in your heart, so that you can do it.
>
> (Deut. 30:11, 14)

There can be no doubt that the reforms of Josiah were met with
popular support. The rank and file of Jerusalem's people chafed, like the
king, under any similance of Assyrian domination, and thus Josiah's initiatives in purging all foreign influences from Judah's life could only be
greeted enthusiastically. In addition, the more thoughtful among Jerusalem's citizens, struck by the disintegration of the most powerful organ-
ism within their world, must have felt the same uneasiness over the
future of Near Eastern civilization which seized their neighbors and by
a similar nostalgia for the past. In Egypt the Pharaohs aped the cultural
achievements of the Old and Middle Kingdoms of more than a thousand

years before. The Babylonians, unsure of their destiny even as they
lurched toward freedom, began to mimic the older Babylonians. And in
Ninevah herself, Ashurbanipal, perhaps the most literate of all the Assyrian monarchs, had established one of the great libraries of antiquity,
and stocked it with copies of ancient texts. Therefore, these reforms of
Josiah which looked back to the grand days of Israel's covenant birth at
Sinai and to the leadership of the midwife of that birth, Moses, found a
ready and receptive mood in the spirit of the people.

It is less certain, however, that the moral and ethical aspects of the
Reformation found as great an acceptance as did its liturgical dimensions.
Personal attitudes and behavior have generally proved more difficult to
change than life's external contours, and this occasion was doubtless no
exception. And yet, even here, there was surely a certain degree of moral
cartharsis on the part of a people who felt themselves to be living at an
important juncture in history.

The Writing of the "Great History"[9]

The years following 621 offer another evidence that many of the
ideals of Josiah's reforms had settled in upon the land. Inspired by the
Book of the Law which Hilkiah had carried from the Temple to the
palace, a vast and probing history of the people of God was begun, a
compendium which was intended to complete their story from the days
of Moses and the Law to the present.

This was not Israel's first effort at writing her history, by any means.
As long ago as the time of David, almost four centuries before, an unknown genius who lived and worked among the Jerusalem scribes (and
whom distant generations would call "the Yahwist," because of his favorite name for God) had collected and arranged stories of Israel's past,
tales going back to the very beginning of human life, and had brilliantly
illuminated these by his own inspired commentary. Not long after that
another craftsman of the pen, one living at the royal court of Solomon,
wove together the exciting saga of the last years of the reign of King
David and the bloody succession to the throne of his son Solomon; an
authentic, objective writing of history a half millennium before Herodotus earned the title "Father of History" and perhaps the first such effort
in human life. And in both northern and southern halves of the Hebrew
nation, men had collected mentally, as well as in written form, tales of
physical and spiritual adventure peculiar to their regions, but illustrating
the experience of Israel as a whole.

Thus the Jerusalem historians, working in the years after 621, had
not only the examples of their predecessors but also, in many cases, material from their hands which they incorporated into their own grand

epic of Israel's life. Their masterpiece was later to form the basis of the
biblical books of Joshua, Judges, Samuel, and Kings, and it was remarkable not simply for its scope and breadth, but also for that particular
interpretation it gave to the drama of Israel's past. Taking its cue directly from the ideals of Josiah's Book of the Law, the new history insisted that Israel's moments of political and economic grandeur invariably
coincided with her times of faithfulness to God and his Laws. When the
people of God sinned, they suffered. When they were morally responsible
and loyal to God, they were prosperous and free. It was as uncomplicated
as that.

> If you will fear the LORD and serve him and hearken to his voice and not
> rebel against the commandment of the LORD, and if both you and the
> king who reigns over you will follow the LORD your God, it will be well;
> but if you will not hearken to the voice of the LORD, but rebel against the
> commandment of the LORD, then the hand of the LORD will be against
> you and your king.
>
> (1 Sam. 12:14f.)

The king, indeed, had a remarkable and singular role to play in
Israel's life, in the eyes of the Josianic historians. As the anointed deputy
of God, the monarch stood under a unique imperative to lead the nation
down broad avenues of piety and devotion and to sustain the moral and
ethical quality of her life upon its most lofty peaks. That monarch who
pursued this commission was held in sacred memory.

> And he [King Hezekiah] did what was right in the eyes of the LORD, ac-
> cording to all that David his father had done. He removed the high places
> [of idolatrous worship], and broke the pillars, and cut down the Asherah.
> And he broke in pieces the bronze serpent that Moses had made, for until
> those days the people of Israel had burned incense to it; it was called
> Nehushtan. He trusted in the LORD the God of Israel. . . . He held fast
> to the LORD; he did not depart from following him, but kept the com-
> mandments which the LORD commanded Moses. And the LORD was with
> him; wherever he went forth, he prospered.
>
> (2 Kings 18:3f.)

But that king who did not respond to the spiritual canons of his office
fell condemned.

> Manasseh was twelve years old when he began to reign. . . . And he did
> what was evil in the sight of the Lord. . . . For he rebuilt the high places
> which Hezekiah his father had destroyed; and he erected altars for Baal,
> and he made an Asherah. . . . And the LORD said by his servants the
> prophets, "Because Manasseh king of Judah has committed these abomina-
> tions, . . . I am bringing upon Jerusalem and Judah such evil that the
> ears of everyone who hears of it will tingle."
>
> (2 Kings 21:1f.)

This grand history was, therefore, more than a history. It was also a
sermon for the times, just as was the Book of the Law which inspired it.

Under Josiah, Judah had charted a new course. A freshly authentic relationship to God was being asserted at the same time that a new freedom and political power were being thrust into Jerusalem's hands. This was no accident, according to the new historians; it was the work of God. And if Judah wished to continue to enjoy liberty and prosperity, she must respond to the Law's demand for the authentic worship of God and for the just and merciful treatment by each man of his neighbor.

The writers of the Great History left no doubt where their political sympathies lay. The very last sentences of the first edition of their work eulogize Josiah and the principles of the Reformation in an unreserved manner. Summarizing all that the king had done, the historians insisted that it was in order that Josiah

> might establish the words of the law which were written in the book that Hilkiah the priest found in the house of the LORD. Before him there was no king like him, who turned to the LORD with all his heart and with all his soul and with all his might, according to the law of Moses. . . .
>
> (2 Kings 23:24f.)

The Death of Josiah and the Resulting Crisis of the Spirit

To what heights Josiah's Reformation might ultimately have soared we shall never know. For in 609, a dozen years after the discovery of the Book of the Law, the sword of Pharaoh Neco of Egypt took the life of the Judean king and murdered, as well, the spiritual and political hopes which were vested in him.

Neco was, at the time, hurrying to the aid of the beleaguered Assyrians, hard pressed at Haran by the Babylonian army of Nabopolassar following the collapse of Nineveh. The Judeans correctly saw in the Egyptian sweep to the north more than simple sympathy by Neco for the Assyrians; they understood that it was also a naked effort to plant Egyptian squadrons and Egyptian tax collectors in the lands of Palestine and Syria. And thus a martial Josiah, who had successfully declared independence from Assyria and who had no intention of yielding to a new master, intercepted the Egyptians at the important crossroads town of Megiddo.

It was no contest. Outmanned by the superior Egyptian army, the Judean force was scattered and Josiah himself was killed (2 Kings

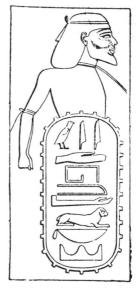

Figure 9. Egyptian Representation of a Hebrew Prisoner.

Figure 10. Egyptian Chariot.

23:29f.). And as the royal chariot bore the torn body of the king back to Jerusalem, all Judah sensed that the dark clouds which had suddenly obscured the sun signalled the approach of violent storms.

The winds and the rains were not long in descending. As soon as Jerusalem could pull herself together from the shock of Josiah's death, the city proclaimed with a brave show of pretended joy the coronation of the dead king's son, Jehoahaz. Yet neither the young ruler nor his demoralized people had any stomach for a prolonged contest with Egypt, nor, for that matter, did they own the resources. As Egyptian armies wrestled with the Babylonians in the north, Neco asserted his mastery over all the lands which touched the western Mediterranean shore, Jerusalem included. And after a brief reign of only three months, Jehoahaz was deposed by Neco and carried away as a captive into Egypt, there to remain until his death. In his place, the Pharaoh enthroned another of Josiah's sons, Jehoiakim, and upon the new king Neco laid the same heavy hand of taxation and tribute which Jehoiakim's predecessors had painfully endured from the Assyrians.[10]

Meanwhile, the death of Josiah had become the occasion for a crisis of the spirit for the obvious reason that the theological foundations which had supported the Reformation of 621 had received very damaging blows. If a right relationship with God was the key to Judah's freedom and prosperity, as the king had vigorously affirmed, how could one now explain the brutal death of the very embodiment of Judah's trust in God and the accompanying loss of her liberty and her fortune? What reason could men now advance for supposing that there was any connection at all between matters of faith and morality, on the one hand, and the political and economic destiny of the people of God, on the other? Did not the tragic and cruel death of the king give the lie to the very principles for which he had lived? These were not easy questions to answer, but to fail to answer them would have been to consent to the darkness which now lurked in Judah's heart. And so men bravely tried to fire the torch.

The spokesmen for the Book of the Law and for the Reformation to which that Law had lent so much impetus argued that Judah's present distress was not a contradiction of faith, however much it might seem so. The horrible truth, as they viewed it, was that the evils which Judah allowed during the long years of her submission to Assyria were so great that not even the piety which had flourished with Josiah was sufficient to compensate. And for that evil Judah was presently being called to account. In a plaintive appendix to the Great History which had been spawned by the Reformation of 621, the long, troublesome reign of Manasseh (Josiah's predecessor, an Assyrian puppet) is recalled, and on the basis of that reign a moral justification for Josiah's death is entered. Although the words were probably written some time after the final collapse of Jerusalem before Babylonian armies, they nevertheless reflect the agonized conclusion to which some were forced by the tragedy of Josiah's death.

> Still the LORD did not turn from the fierceness of his great wrath, by which his anger was kindled against Judah, because of all the provocations with which Manasseh had provoked him. And the LORD said, "I will remove Judah also out of my sight, as I have removed Israel, and I will cast off this city which I have chosen, Jerusalem, and the house of which I said, My name shall be there."
>
> (2 Kings 23:26f.)

But another, more profound answer to the crisis was to come from Jeremiah of Anathoth.[11] Although Jeremiah had been an outspoken critic of Judah's idolatry during the years before Josiah's Reformation, the fiery young spokesman for the God of Israel had grown quiet in the years following 621. As he watched the purging of the Temple of its idols and its rededication to the pure traditions of Israel's ancient covenant, the hope was kindled in Jeremiah that an accompanying reformation of Judah's heart would transpire also, a rededication to the ideals of mercy and justice for which the old Book of the Law had so eloquently pled.

Yet, with the passing of the years, it grew upon Jeremiah that the external aspects of Josiah's Reformation were accorded more sincere treatment than were its internal, moral dimensions. With eagerness many men and women greeted the renewed emphasis upon Temple worship and that special relationship between God and Judah which that worship implied. It neatly dovetailed into the kindled patriotism of the moment and offered snug comfort in the chill political winds which were blowing throughout the ancient Near East. Armed thus with a right relationship with God, they reasoned, what ill could now befall the Lord's own people?

Less eagerly, however, did Judah embrace the lofty ethical demands to which Josiah's Reformation called her. To Jeremiah it seemed that the poor and the distressed were frequently ignored by the very people who fell over one another getting into the Temple for worship. And with sorrow he noted that thievery, adultery, and a low regard for human life still were to be found among God's own people.

It may be that, even before Josiah's violent death, Jeremiah's conscience had compelled him to speak out against the artificial twist which the king's reforms had taken. But certainly, with the death of the king and with the whole future of the Reformation in jeopardy over the shattering of many of its basic assumptions, Jeremiah could no longer keep silent. Shortly after Jehoiakim ascended the Judean throne, Jeremiah stood in the entrance to the Temple and proclaimed in a commanding voice:

> Hear the Word of the LORD, all you men of Judah who enter these gates to worship the LORD. Thus says the LORD of hosts, the God of Israel, Amend your ways and your doings, and I will let you dwell in this place. Do not trust in these deceptive words: 'This is the temple of the LORD, the temple of the LORD, the temple of the LORD.'
>
> For if you truly amend your ways and your doings, if you truly execute justice one with another, if you do not oppress the alien, the fatherless or the widow, or shed innocent blood in this place, and if you do not go after other gods to your own hurt, then I will let you dwell in this place, in the land that I gave of old to your fathers for ever.
>
> Behold, you trust in deceptive words to no avail. Will you steal, murder, commit adultery, swear falsely, burn incense to Baal, and go after other gods that you have not known, and then come and stand before me in this house, which is called by my name, and say, 'We are delivered!'—only to go on doing all these abominations? Has this house, which is called by my name, become a den of robbers in your eyes? Behold, I myself have seen it, says the LORD. Go now to my place that was in Shiloh, where I made my name dwell at first, and see what I did to it for the wickedness of my people Israel. And now, because you have done all these things, says the LORD, and when I spoke to you persistently you did not listen, and when I called you, you did not answer, therefore I will do to the house which is called by my name, and in which you trust, and to the place which I gave to you and to your fathers, as I did to Shiloh.
>
> (Jer. 7:2–14; cf. 26:1–6)

The response of Jeremiah's hearers to this sermon is significant not only because it mirrors the current mood of Jerusalem's people and reveals how far they had strayed from the ideals of Josiah's Reformation, but it also sets the tone for the treatment Jeremiah was to expect for the rest of his life. No sooner had the prophet finished speaking than there was a small riot. Temple officials and by-standing worshippers raised such a clamor of protest that members of the royal court rushed from Jehoiakim's nearby palace to restore order, and it was only their intervention which saved Jeremiah from the mob's murderous designs.

The prophet's reply to the spiritual crisis occasioned by Josiah's death in 609 was thus that of an uncompromising demand for moral obedience to God. There is no suggestion in the preaching of Jeremiah that he opposed the ministrations of the Temple priests, so central to Josiah's reforms, or that he felt that the ritual practiced in the House of God was detrimental to Judah's life. Rather, it was a simple matter of priorities. To the prophet's mind the worship of God was of no benefit, no matter how pure its forms, unless it led to a sharpened awareness of moral and social obligation on the part of both the individual and the nation. If justice and mercy live, so will Judah. If not, Jerusalem will become a desolation like Shiloh, the old Hebrew shrine destroyed by the Philistines which had stood in ruins these four centuries.

There is another aspect of Jeremiah's faith, a private aspect, which went beyond and at the same time supported his public affirmation. That was his conviction that a man or woman must stand in dutiful obedience before God, responding to God's moral and spiritual demands, even though God offers no immediate hope of benefit from that obedience whatsoever. This insistence upon radical compliance with the will of God represents Jeremiah's sharpest divergence from the ideals of Josiah's Reformation. In this regard, the prophet's life more than his words offers the sermon, as the following incidents reveal.

At an early age, when most young Judean men were assuming for themselves the joys and responsibilities of a family, it became clear to Jeremiah that he could never marry. The reason, as he later explained, was that the demands of his calling from God were too great to be laid, even in a partial manner, upon the shoulders of wife and children (Jer. 16:1–13). On numerous later occasions, including that of his "Temple Sermon" of 609, Jeremiah knew that to speak the words which God had planted in his heart would result in great suffering on his part, perhaps even death (Jer. 38:15). Most significantly of all, when Jerusalem later fell to Babylonian armies, as Jeremiah had promised, the prophet found himself in the hands of the enemy. The Babylonian officer treated Jeremiah kindly and offered him asylum from the anger of his countrymen. But Jeremiah refused the Babylonian hospitality and remained in a hos-

tile Judah because his people were there and because God had yet further work for him to do among them (Jer. 40:1–6).

It should not be assumed from this that the prophet from Anathoth
was determined to be a martyr. Jeremiah loved life as much as anyone
and, as a deeply perceptive and sensitive man, he responded to the beau-
ties of nature and to the joys of human existence. His lust for life, in
fact, often collided with his prophetic calling. Then, as can only a man
who takes the divine imperatives with total and unreserved seriousness,
Jeremiah wrestled with God, cursing the day of his birth (Jer. 15:10),
threatening to run away to the desert (Jer. 9:2), and even spitting these
emotions into God's face:

> O Lord, thou hast deceived me,
>   and I was deceived;
> thou art stronger than I,
>   and thou hast prevailed.
> I have become a laughingstock all the day;
>   every one mocks me.
> For whenever I speak, I cry out,
>   I shout, "Violence and destruction!"
> For the word of the Lord has become for me
>   a reproach and a derision all day long.
>   (Jer. 20:7f.)

Yet Jeremiah was captive to that word of the Lord, a word which, on
another occasion, he called "a joy and a delight of my heart" (Jer. 15:16).
And, as far as is known, he never failed to respond when it was directed
to him nor failed God's commission to speak it to others.

Thus, it was in Jeremiah's personal life, as much as in his speech, that
his faith and spiritual vision were on display. Judah must respond in
moral obedience to the urgings of God simply because she is God's people and he has come to her in his love. If she obeys, she will live; but her
obedience should not be motivated by that hope. Judah should obey God
simply as an act of loving response to his compassion for her, as had
Jeremiah himself, regardless of what form the consequence might take.
It was a faith which promised no benefits but the gift of itself!

The Reaction Under Jehoiakim

The new king lost no time in casting his political and spiritual shadow
across Judah's life. Whether he sheltered strong Egyptian sympathies, we
have no way of knowing, but willingly or not, Jehoiakim permitted his
kingdom to be drawn ever more tightly into the Egyptian orbit. In the
king's defense it must be pointed out that a pro-Egyptian stance on the

part of Judah was not without a certain strong logic, and such a posture must have appealed to a number of thoughtful citizens of Jerusalem, including many influential members of the royal court. A compelling case could be made, in projecting the scenario for the future, that in this world of vast and muscular empires there was no longer a place for an independent Judah. Only in docile alliance with some virile power could the nation obtain security and prosperity, and with Egypt so near, that nation offered the best hope for Judah's tomorrow.

Therefore, in spite of the wounds to her pride and purse as an Egyptian vassal, Judah settled down to accommodate herself to a new life. The shock of Josiah's death and its accompanying spiritual agony began softly to recede and some of the sweetness of life returned. The sunshine and rain still descended from heaven, the fig and grape yet came to fruit, and the cycle of birth, marriage and death went on. The fighting was far to the north and, as no Judean blood was being spilled, it was only of marginal consequence to Jerusalem. And so, with the return to her life of regularity and order, Jerusalem settled into a bland contentment. Pagan and idolatrous practices crept back into the Temple worship and into local shrines across the countryside. And as for the moral code which the Book of the Law had grandly championed, it was all but forgotten.

Only that vestige of the Reformation which catered to Judah's self interest was retained, that one element in all that Josiah had worked for which now soothed Jerusalem's falsely tranquil soul. Yet not even Josiah would have recognized it now for it was, in fact, a parody of the ideals of 621. It was the insistence that, because the Jerusalem Temple was the House of God, no ultimate evil could befall the city or its people. Weaving in and out among the shrines and altars of the Temple, the unctuous prophets of the cult smoothly chanted their false oracles from God.

Figure 11. A Stable Scene from an Assyrian Relief.

> You shall not see the sword, nor shall you have famine, but I will give
> you assured peace in this place.
>
> (Jer. 14:13)

As an example of the decadence of the early years of Jehoiakim's
reign, the new king pulled down large sections of the royal palace, portions of which had stood for more than three centuries, and caused them
to be rebuilt to a more luxurious scale than ever before. Grand salons,
panelled in cedar and ornamented with murals and tapestries, were provided by the king for himself. And when the royal treasury ran thin because of these heavy expenditures, Jehoiakim impressed Judean citizens
to work upon the project as his virtual slaves.

These events did not, to be sure, go unresisted. The scribes who had
written the Great History were still to be found in their schools, reflecting upon the course of current events with the increasingly small audi-
ences who would listen. And independent prophets of the stripe of Jeremiah publicly decried an attitude toward life and toward God which,
they insisted, could lead only to destruction.

One of these was a man from the Judean village of Kiriath-jearim
named Uriah (Jer. 26:20–23). After lashing out at the moral and spiritual
paralysis which claimed his country, Uriah was approached by officers of
the king and, fearing for his life, fled to Egypt. But the hapless prophet
had chosen the wrong sanctuary, for the Egyptians gleefully surrendered
him to Jehoiakim's emissaries, who carted him back to Jerusalem. There,
in the presence of the king, Uriah was impaled upon a sword and his
body thrown into a pauper's grave.

But the most decisive voice of all raised against the tenor of these
early years of Jehoiakim continued to be that of Jeremiah. Undeterred
by the fate of Uriah and by his own narrow brush with death, he leveled
a damning indictment against Jehoiakim for the king's wanton display
of extravagance and waste in building a new palace (Jer. 22:13–19). Re-
minding the monarch of the superb example of compassion and justice
set by his own father, for whom the old palace had been quite good
enough, Jeremiah wanted to know if Jehoiakim was now any more of a
king because of his splendid lodgings or because of the brutality and
oppression by which they had been built. Of course he was not, intoned
the prophet. He was less of a king. And to prove the fact, God would
lead him to death in disgrace. There would be no sorrow at his passing,
and his burial would be like that of a common ass, with his carcass hauled
outside the city wall and tossed upon a rubbish heap!

It was about this time that Pashur, a priestly official at the Temple,
had Jeremiah arrested, beaten, and locked overnight in the stocks in a
public place where all could stare and jeer (Jer. 20:1–6).

Judah Becomes a Babylonian Vassal

When the news arrived in Jerusalem in 605 that the armies of Pharaoh Neco had suffered a crushing defeat at Carchemish, the reaction may not have been immediate. But as the Egyptian combat detachments and their battalions of supply reeled painfully southward, many of them passing not far from Jerusalem, the awareness dawned that Judah was about to be exposed to a new threat. And when neighboring Ashkelon fell to Nebuchadrezzar's fighters in the following year, after a bloody siege, it was clear to Jehoiakim that his reliance upon Egypt was, for now at least, at an end. We do not know precisely when or in what manner Jerusalem fell into the hands of the Babylonians, but it was presumably at about the time of the siege of Ashkelon that an advancing Babylonian column arrived before the walls of the city and demanded submission. As Neco was now in headlong flight and Jehoiakim was without a significant military force of his own, a defenseless Jerusalem had no recourse but to comply. And with hardly an unsheathed sword, the captains of Nebuchadrezzar entered the Sheep Gate and, quickly finding their way to the royal apartments, disarmed the palace guard.

There was remarkably little fuss about it all. For one thing, the Babylonians had bigger fish to fry, namely the Egyptian army which should be crushed before it could withdraw behind the safety of its own border fortifications. And secondly, the Babylonians wanted money, not blood, and they took the latter only if the former were denied. Thus after depositing with Jehoiakim a statement for his expected contribution to the Babylonian exchequer, they went away, leaving sufficient patrols in the neighborhood to remind the Judeans where their new allegiances lay. Jerusalem's changed status was, therefore, largely an administrative matter. To the farmer plowing his fields under the blue Judean sky or to the shopkeeper selling his wares in the crowded, noisy marketplace, the transition made little, if any, difference at all. Taxes remained outrageously high; but whether they lined the pockets of Neco or of Nebuchadrezzar was irrelevant to the concerns of daily life. And if it were not for the occasional glimpses of Babylonian soldiers riding through the countryside or strolling calmly down the twisted lanes and alleys of old Jerusalem, one would never have guessed that the Egyptians had gone away.

To certain of the king's counselors, however, perhaps even to Jehoiakim himself, the Babylonian control of Jerusalem was a distasteful dose. Few who were attentive to such matters felt that Neco had left the field of battle for good. Egypt's ruler was a proud and pugnacious man and, having reached the sanctuary of the Nile, he would now be bandaging his wounds and calculating revenge. Many who were entrusted with

Judah's leadership feared that, when the day came for Neco to venture from his lair, Jerusalem herself might become the theater in which his contest with Nebuchadrezzar would be renewed. In addition, many of these advisors to the king entertained a simple and reasonable bias in Egypt's favor. It was difficult for them to believe that Nebuchadrezzar could maintain a position of strength in southern Palestine, so close to the borders of Egypt. To those who pointed to the example of Assyria, which had managed that very feat for a century, they cockily replied that Nebuchadrezzar was no Sargon. The time would come when Egypt would strike, they insisted, and Jerusalem must be ready to seize the opportunity such an offensive would offer to her. Therefore, Jehoiakim and his court dutifully sent their gold and silver to Babylon, listening, all the while, for the slightest rustle of arms to the south.

In the meantime, Jeremiah continued to be Jehoiakim's *bête noire*, a tenacious and eloquent party of opposition on two feet. As long before as the early years of Josiah, Jeremiah had talked in grim tones about a "foe from the north" who would become the machine by which God would punish his people for their sins (Jer. 1:14f.). Jeremiah had not been very precise about the matter at the time and, since few people paid attention to him anyway, no one bothered to ask for clarification. And during those blissful years after 621, Jeremiah himself seems to have let the matter drop. But following the death of Josiah, Jeremiah revived his talk about a northern avenger sent by God.

Figure 12. Dragon in Enamelled Brick from the Ishtar Gate, Babylon.

Blow the trumpet through the land;
   cry aloud and say,
"Assemble, and let us go
   into the fortified cities!"
Raise a standard toward Zion,
   flee for safety, stay not,
for I bring evil from the north,
   and great destruction.
A lion has gone up from his thicket,
   a destroyer of nations has set out;
   he has gone forth from his place
to make your land a waste;
   your cities will be ruins
   without inhabitant.

                (Jer. 4:5–7; cf. 6:1, 22; 10:22)

Perhaps the identity of the "foe from the north" was not clear even to Jeremiah in those early years. His forebodings regarding Jerusalem's destruction may have been stimulated, in part, by the general disquiet in the ancient Near East that the established order was about to collapse, to the detriment of civilized men everywhere. But following Carchemish and Ashkelon and the gentle capitulation of Jerusalem, Jeremiah began to identify the avenger of God as Nebuchadrezzar himself. He was to be the whip with which God would scourge Judah, the lion that would devour her body. As for Egypt, she herself would be butchered by Babylonian swordsmen, and those who were tempted to look to her for help would look in vain (Jer. 46).

Quite naturally Jehoiakim, who had already learned to loathe Jeremiah, hated him all the more bitterly for this brazen audacity, and he pronounced the prophet *persona non grata*. No longer was he allowed to enter the city or to worship at the Temple. If he must speak, he could do so to those country fellows in Anathoth where no harm could come of his words. Yet even Jeremiah's townsmen had been infected against him, for when he returned to his ancestral home, he was threatened with death if he should so much as open his mouth (Jer. 11:21).

Jeremiah, who would not be silent in the face of God's command to speak, went and hid among the rocks and stones of the wilderness and summoned to his side his trusted scribe, Baruch, ordering the man to transcribe the salient features of his prophetic message (Jer. 36:1–32). Baruch was then directed to return with the scroll to Jerusalem and to be alert for some especially pertinent occasion to read Jeremiah's words to the people. Several months later, as Babylonian armies made their initial approach toward the city and Judeans for miles around gathered anxiously in the Temple to fast and pray, Baruch stood up. In a voice which filled the Temple courtyard, he recited Jeremiah's words from God: his indictment of Judah's sin and his promise of divine chastisement at the hand of Jerusalem's enemies.

In the reaction which ensued, Baruch was relieved of the scroll by a group of royal officials who then carried it into the presence of the king, where Jeremiah's words were read again. And as each section was completed, the furious Jehoiakim ripped it from the scroll with a knife and threw it into a glowing brazier. But Baruch, once more safely with Jeremiah, made a second copy of Jeremiah's oracles which damned Jehoiakim even more blackly than had the first.

Jehoiakim Revolts

The pro-Egyptian faction in Jehoiakim's court was elated when, in 601, Pharaoh Neco sallied out beyond his own borders and, at the head of a formidable Egyptian force, advanced into southern Palestine. Nebuchadrezzar was waiting for him and the two armies hacked away at one another amid a rising pool of human blood. At sunset the cream of the Babylonian military lay dead or dying and a cursing Nebuchadrezzar was in a hasty, if orderly, retreat to the north. When the news reached Jerusalem, bonfires kindled on the city walls shared the good news with the Judean countryside. Jehoiakim and his advisors lost no time in repudiating their vassalage to Nebuchadrezzar, and the token Babylonian force in the city was quickly overcome and butchered.

Nebuchadrezzar was too busily occupied with repairing his military machine to respond immediately to Jehoiakim's impudence. The best he could do for the moment was to loose certain of Judah's neighbors upon her, people who, in spite of the Egyptian show of force, had retained their Babylonian allegiances. Thus for a time roving bands of Ammonites, Moabites, and others harassed the outlying areas of the Judean countryside, rendering rural life uncomfortable and perilous (2 Kings 24:2). But Jehoiakim remained defiant of Nebuchadrezzar, even as he cast hopeful glances toward Egypt that Neco would aid his rebellion or, barring that, would at least leave Jerusalem undisturbed to pursue her own destiny.

In his exile, Jeremiah could scarcely contain himself, and he lost no time in describing to Jehoiakim the consequences of his foolish insurgency.

> Therefore thus says the Lord of hosts: Because you have not obeyed my words, behold, I will send for all the tribes of the north, says the Lord, and for Nebuchadrezzar the king of Babylon, my servant, and I will bring them against this land and its inhabitants, and against all these nations round about; I will utterly destroy them, and make them a horror, a hissing, and an everlasting reproach.
>
> (Jer. 25:8f.)

It was words like these which convinced Jehoiakim and many other men of responsibility that Jeremiah was a traitor to his country, one who wished to see Judah lose her freedom to a Babylonian overlord. And it is not difficult to understand how the prophet's enemies should have come to that conclusion, for his words flirted perilously close to sedition. But Jeremiah was later to prove, especially in his refusal of the Babylonian offer of sanctuary, that his only concern was for Judah's welfare. The prophet was animated by the conviction that God had chosen Babylon as the vehicle by which to bring thoughtless and sinful Judah to her senses, and all efforts to frustrate the divine will could merely postpone the eventual day of reckoning. But the king and those who sat in the councils of state were, at the moment, largely unconcerned with whatever it was that Jeremiah might be thinking, for they were sure that the tides of fortune were rising to their advantage.

It is strange that Neco did not attempt to consolidate the Egyptian victory of 601. A bold march up the eastern Mediterranean coast at that juncture would presumably have exposed large areas of Babylonian colonial territory to the Pharaoh's claims and deprived Nebuchadrezzar of badly needed sources of revenue. As it was, only Judah seems to have wrenched herself out of the Babylonian grasp while, to the south, Neco and his army were content to maintain a low and indistinct profile. Perhaps the Pharaoh's own losses argued against such offensive action. Or perhaps Neco's clash with Nebuchadrezzar was only a defensive effort on the Egyptians' part to forestall an invasion of the Nile valley, as the Babylonian Chronicle suggests, and that following the successful completion of the battle, the Pharaoh was satisfied to retire behind his own frontiers once again, congratulating himself that they were now more secure than ever.

However it may have been, Nebuchadrezzar appears not to have made a major military move for three years, a period, the Babylonian Chronicle instructs us, in which he was busily beefing up his armed forces. When he did take the offensive again, his target, as Jeremiah had dolefully predicted, was Jerusalem. In December of the year 598, the initial wave of a large Babylonian force put itself in readiness to leave the banks of the Euphrates and to set a course for Judah. Nebuchadrezzar had rightly calculated that southern Palestine would never be securely his again until Jehoiakim's capital was humbled. But scarcely had the Babylonian cavalry and foot paraded through the great Ishtar Gate in a colorful farewell to home than the news arrived from Jerusalem that King Jehoiakim was dead.

Chapter Three

*In the seventh year [i.e., 598 B.C.], the month
of Kislev, the king of Akkad mustered his troops,
marched to the Hatti-land,
And encamped against the city of Judah, and on the
second day of the month Adar he seized the
city and captured the king.
He appointed there a king of his own choice,
received its heavy tribute, and sent it to
Babylon.*

—The Babylonian Chronicle

Jehoiachin Submits to Nebuchadrezzar

It is possible to speculate, but not to prove, that the adolescent son of
Jehoiakim who now inherited the throne of David was a capable and
compelling person. Jehoiachin had first seen the light of a Jerusalem sun
only eighteen years before, during those halcyon days of his grandfather's
Reformation. And the length of time from his accession to the arrival of
the first Babylonian troops before Jerusalem's walls could hardly have
been more than three to four weeks. Yet in spite of his youth and in spite
of the abruptness with which crucial decisions were thrust upon him,
Jehoiachin seems to have exercised a prudence—although some would

Figure 13. Siege with Battering Rams. An Assyrian Stone Carving.

have said a cowardice—which surpassed by far that of his father Jehoiakim
and that of his uncle Zedekiah, who would succeed him as Judah's ruler.
Although he did not rehabilitate the reforms of Josiah (a fact which
would later earn him a scornful notice from the historians of the school
of the Book of the Law (2 Kings 24:9), he did prove himself less susceptible to the wiles of the pro-Egyptian lobby at court which had exercised
so strong an influence upon his father. And he thereby saved his country
and himself much suffering.

On the 16th of March, 597, barely two months into the Babylonian
siege of Jerusalem, Jehoiachin surrendered his city and submitted himself to the mercy of Nebuchadrezzar. It is possible that the young king
had been influenced by the opinions of Jeremiah, preachments of which
he was surely vividly aware. Or perhaps the experience of Ashkelon, seven
years before, with its cost in human suffering and physical destruction,
weighed heavily upon Jehoiachin. At any rate, the new king seems to
have calculated a certain flinty reasonableness from Nebuchadrezzar, and
he received precisely that. Following the capitulation of the city, Jehoiachin and his mother, Jehoiakim's former queen, were carried captive to
Babylon, along with sizable numbers of the royal household. The Temple
and the royal palace were looted of their gold, silver, and precious stones.
And a large contingent of soldiers, bureaucrats, and skilled craftsmen, together with their families, was taken into exile in Babylon.

Yet, as Jehoiachin must have sensed, the devastation could have been
much worse. In spite of his captivity from which he never returned, the
king and his household were treated with decorum and respect. Cuneiform documents have been recovered which list Jehoiachin's ample rations in captivity;[12] and later, upon the death of Nebuchadrezzar, the
exiled Jewish king was to be elevated to a place of honor in the banquet-
ing hall of the new Babylonian sovereign, Amel-Marduk (2 Kings 25:27f.).
As for the Temple and the palace, although deprived of their finest appointments, these buildings remained intact, the one a continuing center
for the worship of God, the other a focal point for Judah's ongoing
political integrity under a new ruler whom Nebuchadrezzar would now
appoint, Zedekiah, the third of Josiah's sons to rule over the city of
David. Also left standing virtually unscathed were the city walls.

With regard to the exiles, it is certain that Judah lost many of her
more valuable citizens. Yet the statement of the historians of the Book of
the Law that no one remained "except the poorest people of the land"
(2 Kings 24:14) must be read as hyperbole, in view of the relative ease
with which Zedekiah was shortly to galvanize the energies of the nation.

In brief, although the rebellion against Babylon fostered by Jehoiakim
was painfully expensive to Jerusalem, it would have cost even more had

Jehoiakim lived to follow his policies to their disastrous conclusion. There is no evidence to suggest that the king was murdered to appease Nebuchadrezzar, as has been speculated. Yet Jehoiakim's death did have the very useful effect of opening the door to the more flexible policies of his son, so that, for the moment at least, total calamity was forestalled. It is perhaps a tribute to Jehoiachin's courage in making a very difficult choice that, for as long as he lived, some Jews considered him their rightful king. Fragments of pottery unearthed in Palestine show that his name was still being inscribed upon some royal properties after his deposition. And a fellow exile, the prophet Ezekiel, dates the first of his visions on a time scale reckoned from Jehoiachin's captivity (Ezek. 1:2).

Zedekiah Begins to Rule

The hatred for the Babylonians by many of Judah's peoples was motivated, of course, by their thirst for freedom. Perhaps if Assyrian domination of Palestine had been immediately followed by the reimposition of force from some other quarter, say from Egypt or from Babylon, continued vassalage would have been accepted by Jerusalem with less truculence, for under the Assyrians she had almost grown accustomed to a servile station. But during the decade and a half between the fall of Nineveh in 626 and the death of Josiah in 609 Judah had grown to enjoy her independence. And so if the behavior upon the throne of the two sons of Josiah who sat there for any significant duration, Jehoiakim and Zedekiah, reveals a rational purpose at all, it is that, although they remained insensitive to their father's spiritual ideals, they and the counselors upon whom they relied for judgment had contracted Josiah's contagious lust for freedom. But whereas the Judah of Josiah had been permitted to gratify its cravings for liberty, the Judah of Jehoiakim and of Zedekiah was not so allowed. And the tragedy which these monarchs brought upon their people resulted in no small measure from their inability to grasp the basic distinction between their father's opportunities and their own.

Zedekiah was scarcely older than his nephew Jehoiachin when Nebuchadrezzar ordered him to assume the vacant chair of David. The Babylonian lord apparently felt, for reasons best known to himself, that the perpetuation of the ancient Judean dynasty offered the best hope for a docile and cooperative Jewish people. And as the eldest of Jehoiachin's sons was either unborn or still in his infancy (1 Chron. 3:17), the third son of Josiah seemed a logical choice to preside over a chastened Jerusalem.

For more than three years following his investiture upon the Judean throne, Zedekiah provided Nebuchadrezzar with little reason to regret his relatively gentle treatment of rebellious Jerusalem. The Babylonian Chronicle soon breaks off and we find ourselves dependent upon the Hebrew Scriptures and upon a few discontinuous fragments of Egyptian and Babylonian material for our understanding of the last crucial years of Judah's life. These lead to the conclusion that Zedekiah initially fulfilled whatever obligations Nebuchadrezzar had imposed upon him, which at minimum included the payment of tribute into the Babylonian monetary chests and the swearing of fealty to Nebuchadrezzar himself. The physical damage inflicted upon the city by two months of siege was soon repaired, perhaps with Babylonian aid; commerce and agriculture began a slow return to normal; and, with a Babylonian military presence scarcely greater than before Jehoiakim's revolt, the routine of business at the royal court moved along smoothly, but cautiously, under the direction of a new king and a new cadre of state officials.

So easily, in fact, did Judah's ship of state resume her natural buoyancy that the feeling crept through the city that the defeat of Jehoiakim's uprising had been a kind of purge which God had imposed upon Jerusalem in order to rid her of her waste. Especially in circles near the new regime, it was reasoned that those who had been carried into exile must have been treated in this manner because they were morally or spiritually inferior to their kinsmen allowed to remain in the land, with the consequence that Jerusalem and Judah were now finer and grander than ever before. Men and women congratulated themselves that, having been spared the judgment, they could look toward the future with a hope whose only uncertainty was a vague imprecision over when and how God's opportunities would arrive. Perhaps there were some who even felt that in the events of 597 the dire warnings of Jeremiah and of Uriah of Kiriath-jearim had been realized. They calculated that now that God had spoken and had inflicted his wrath upon those who genuinely deserved it, the remainder of the nation could be about its business in the conviction that the God of Israel was with them and would see them through whatever tomorrow might bring. It must be remembered, they chanted gently to one another, that Jerusalem is the city of God, the Temple is the place of God, and God was committed to guard that which was his own. Hadn't Josiah himself taught them that?

But into the teeth of this spirit of self-congratulation Jeremiah flung his vision of two baskets of figs (Jer. 24:1–10). In one container the fruit was ripe, plump, and juicy, just the thing to set on one's table. But the figs in the other basket were putrid and rotten, and they emitted a pungent, sickening stench. The good figs are the exiles, said Jeremiah. God will treasure them and restore them to their own land. But the bad figs are Zedekiah, his princely subordinates, and all the remnant of people left in the land. God will do to them what must be done to all bad figs.

> And I will send sword, famine, and pestilence upon them, until they shall be utterly destroyed from the land which I gave to them and their fathers.
> (Jer. 24:10)

But few in Jerusalem's throng were interested in listening to such gloom.

Zedekiah's Seditious Conference

In 594 two events far from Jerusalem stirred considerable interest in the court of King Zedekiah. In Egypt Pharaoh Neco died and was succeeded by his son, Psammetichus II. The older king must have expired in some frustration, because his hopes for reestablishing the ancient Egyptian hegemony over Palestine and Syria had been dashed at Carchemish and, in spite of the battering which he administered to Nebuchadrezzar in the unnamed battle of 601, Neco had never been able to present a serious threat to the Babylonian rule over the region he so coveted. But with Neco's death a new, young heart now beat upon Egypt's throne, and in Jerusalem men wondered aloud what this might portend for Judah's future.

Figure 14. Relief from the Throne of Pharoah Neco.

Even as men of responsibility were quietly pondering this turn of events, news arrived of a recent revolt among the Jewish exiles in Babylon. The details of this affair are quite unclear, but two men who presented themselves as prophets of God, Ahab the son of Kolaiah and Zedekiah the son of Maaseiah (no apparent relation to the Judean king), seem to have fomented trouble among the Babylonian Jews, possibly by a call to arms or at least by the promise of a speedy release from captivity (Jer. 29:21f.). Is this the same domestic rebellion of the year 595 which the authors of the Babylonian Chronicle dignify by a notice in their baked clay annals? We do not know; but, like that insurgency, the rashness of Ahab ben Koliah and Zedekiah ben Maaseiah was brutally suppressed by the Babylonians, for the Jewish would-be prophets were summarily and publicly burned at the stake, the incident attracting attention in Jerusalem and causing the circles around the king to buzz with excited parley.

As a result of one or both of these events, Zedekiah summoned to his court the ambassadors of Edom, Moab, Ammon, Tyre, and Sidon, five neighboring principalities which, like Judah, were vassals of Nebuchadrezzar (Jer. 27:3). The conversation, one may easily assume, centered around the prospects for a successful repudiation of Babylonian power. If rioting in Babylon should occupy Nebuchadrezzar's attentions at home and a military sortie led by the new Pharaoh should pin down Babylonian forces in the south, a coordinated insurrection among several of Nebuchadrezzar's subjects must surely have excellent prospects of success.

But the security which ought to have surrounded so volatile a conference proved to be extremely loose. For one thing, Jeremiah found out about it and lost no time denouncing what he considered to be stupid, even iniquitous intentions. His address to King Zedekiah on this occasion provided the clearest summary of his attitude toward Nebuchadrezzar as an agent of God.

> Thus says the LORD of hosts, the God of Israel: This is what you shall say to your masters: "It is I who by my great power and my outstretched arm have made the earth, with the men and animals that are on the earth, and I give it to whomever it seems right to me. Now I have given all these lands into the hand of Nebuchadnezzar, the king of Babylon, my servant, and I have given him also the beasts of the field to serve him. All the nations shall serve him and his son and his grandson, until the time of his own land comes; then many nations and great kings shall make him their slave. But if any nation or kingdom will not serve this Nebuchadnezzar king of Babylon, and put its neck under the yoke of the king of Babylon, I will punish that nation with the sword, with famine, with pestilence, says the LORD, until I have consumed it by his hand."
>
> (Jer. 27:4–8)

To no one's astonishment, Nebuchadrezzar himself got wind of the seditious meeting and summoned Zedekiah to Babylon in order to give an account of himself (Jer. 51:59). Either the king presented his case quite effectively or Nebuchadrezzar was still in an unusually lenient mood toward Judah, for Zedekiah was given nothing more than a reprimand and allowed to return home. And, as we hear of no more disquiet among the Jews of Babylon and know of no military thrust by Psammetichus II into the south of Palestine, Zedekiah was probably more than happy, for the moment at least, to let the matter drop.

Meanwhile, Jeremiah took a further step to indicate his conviction concerning the direction in which God's will lay (Jer. 29). He wrote a letter to the Babylonian exiles and entrusted it to two friends, who perhaps traveled in Zedekiah's own party to Babylon. In it he advised the deportees to settle down to as near normal a life as their strange surroundings would permit, for God had no word for them which promised an early release, no matter what people like the false prophets Ahab ben Koliah and Zedekiah ben Maaseiah might tell them. Still, they should not give up hope, for God had not forgotten them and would ultimately return them to their homeland.

Zedekiah Revolts

Five years passed before Zedekiah and his fellow conspirators saw in events in Egypt a renewed opportunity to raise once more the bloody shirt of revolt. As in 594, the Jewish aspirations for freedom from Babylonian rule were now vested in yet another new Pharaoh, for, after a brief rule of only half a decade, Psammetichus II died in 589 and was replaced upon the throne by his son Apries, or, as the Old Testament knows him, Hophra (Jer. 44:30). Every indication is that the new Egyptian sovereign, in addition to being young, was also headstrong and rash, and before his rule of two decades was terminated in an angry *coup d'etat* he left a trail of blood from Syria to the western reaches of the Libyan coast. Not long after his accession, Apries dispatched a naval flotilla of armed troop transports to the Phoenician coastal citadel of Tyre and occupied that city and neighboring Sidon. Whether Apries acted in response to a Phoenician request is not known, but, as both Tyrean and Sidonian representatives had attended Zedekiah's seditious conference in Jerusalem in 594, it is possible that the Phoenicians welcomed the Egyptian presence as a means of ridding themselves of their Babylonian masters.

Elsewhere men watched the new Egyptian initiatives and took hope. The Ammonites, who had also attended Zedekiah's Jerusalem meeting, took the opportunity of Pharoah's military activities to withhold tribute from the Babylonians. And in Jerusalem itself strong voices urged upon Zedekiah that the powder of revolt was ready for firing. The king, however, was not yet prepared to light the fuse. He doubtless chafed under the Babylonian bonds as much as anyone, but it had been he who had been forced to stand under the withering gaze of Nebuchadrezzar not long before, and he knew that that monarch's forbearance was not infinite. There could be no revolt unless Jewish arms were perfectly assured of success, and Zedekiah did not yet have that assurance. So the king dallied while his more militant courtiers grew increasingly restive.

As the weeks passed, however, events slowly eroded Zedekiah's cautious posture. For one thing, the Babylonian loss of Tyre and Sidon went unrebuked by Nebuchadrezzar. Babylonian reinforcements moved to the scene and preparations for siege were begun, but, with their flank upon an open sea dotted with Egyptian sails, the Phoenician warriors mocked the Babylonians from the security of their stout stone fortifications. For another thing, in the exchange of embassies between Jerusalem and Memphis, Apries, by lavish promises of Egyptian aid, must certainly have strengthened the hand of those in Zedekiah's court who counseled war. It was in Egypt's every interest to urge a clash of arms between Jew and Babylonian and, parading fat Egyptian promises before Zedekiah's eyes, the king's more martial nobles weakened the royal resolve to pursue a course of peace.

At length Zedekiah caved in, and on an autumn day in 589 armed troops of the king's guard assaulted the Babylonian garrison in Jerusalem and killed or imprisoned its personnel. Judah had thrown down her gauntlet for one last, fatal time.

Nebuchadrezzar Moves Against Jerusalem

When the news arrived that Babylonian troops were on their way to Jerusalem and that Nebuchadrezzar himself was in Syria to direct operations against his rebellious Jewish, Phoenician, and Ammonite subjects and their Egyptian sponsors, Jeremiah brazenly confronted his king in the yard of the Temple. He announced that God had doomed the uprising and that Zedekiah's worst fears of another personal confrontation with Nebuchadrezzar would be realized.

> Thus says the LORD: Behold, I am giving this city into the hand of the king of Babylon, and he shall burn it with fire. You shall not escape from his hand, but shall surely be captured and delivered into his hand; you shall see the king of Babylon eye to eye and speak with him face to face; and you shall go to Babylon.
>
> (Jer. 34:2f.)

Yet Jeremiah seems to have sensed the anguish of the young king, trapped between his own nightmares and the patriotic fervor of his people. And in words which contrast sharply with his bitter vituperation directed against Jehoiakim at the time of that monarch's insurgency, Jeremiah tells Zedekiah plaintively, "You shall not die by the sword. You shall die in peace" (Jer. 34:4f.). It was, at least, some rag of solace.

But if Jeremiah's melancholy warnings dismayed Zedekiah, his spirits were further depressed when, in the early weeks of 588, the Babylonian armies penetrated Judah, quickly devoured most of the outlying fortifications, and dug themselves in for their second siege of Jerusalem within a decade. The combatants on each side were aware that this struggle would be much longer and more deadly than before, and both within and without the city walls preparations were made to sustain human life over a considerable period of time under circumstances of distress and danger. The few couriers who managed to slip through the Babylonian lines into the beleaguered city brought the news that of all Jerusalem's perimeter defenses, only the fortresses at Lachish and Azekah, both to the west, still held out—and they none too certainly. The same couriers, rested and refreshed, were then sent out again, this time in the direction of Egypt, with urgent appeals to Pharaoh Apries for help. Only when a messenger's racked and tortured body was not catapulted back into the surrounded city by one of the great engines of siege could Zedekiah hope that Apries would hear his plea and respond.

The archaeologist's pick has exhumed moving evidence of the pro-

Figure 15. A Prisoner Being Skinned Alive. An Assyrian Stone Carving.

gressive decay of the Judean position in the face of the determined Babylonian efforts to suppress this newest insurgency. In 1935 and 1938 a collection of broken pottery fragments, covered by a faded Hebrew script, was discovered in the ruins of the Jewish fortifications at Lachish.[13] Upon examination, they proved to be letters written to the commander of the Jewish military garrison in that city at the time of the siege of Jerusalem and were apparently sent by the leader of a small force of armed Jews who had taken up positions somewhere between Lachish and Azekah when only these two outposts still stood with Jerusalem against the fury of Nebuchadrezzar. Even as these brave men stood their ground, the lights of their world were being extinguished. In one missive the writer complains that, while the signal fires of Lachish are still visible to him and his party, "we no longer see those of Azekah." In another he refers to a certain military officer named Koniyahu who has gone to Egypt, presumably to implore the Pharaoh's aid. And in yet another of the letters, the writer declares that "the words of the prophet are not good, liable to loosen the hands of the country and the city," an allegation which causes the modern reader to remember the similar charges raised against Jeremiah (cf. Jer. 38:4).

But Lachish soon fell, as had Azekah, and was put to the torch by marauding troops, while the life, or at least the liberty, of the anonymous writer of the pathetic letters on clay went forfeit. The noose around Jerusalem's neck drew ever tighter.

In the city itself men agonized and sought the consolations of religious faith. Special prayers were offered in the Temple and the sacrificial fires burned day and night. Remembering the role of the prophet Isaiah in the days when Jerusalem was surrounded by the Assyrian army of Sennacherib and the remarkable lifting of that siege, the king dispatched a messenger to Jeremiah with the petition that the prophet pray for the city's deliverance (cf. 2 Kings 19). And as a gesture intended to please their God, the citizens of Jerusalem, doubtless at the king's insistence, released their indentured servants—Jews themselves—from all obligations. In truth, many of these slaves, who were used largely for agricultural purposes, were now rendered worthless to their masters by the Babylonian occupation of the outlying countryside and, with food supplies beginning to grow slim, may have constituted an outright liability. Yet the formal act of their release was lacquered over with a thick coating of piety and endless assertions of the masters' good moral and spiritual inclinations. But if anyone was taken in by these pretensions of mercy, he was soon to be disabused of such illusions.

Meanwhile, Koniyahu or one of Zedekiah's other couriers made his way to the court of Pharaoh Apries and impressed upon the Egyptians the urgency of Jerusalem's plight. At some point in the siege, probably in

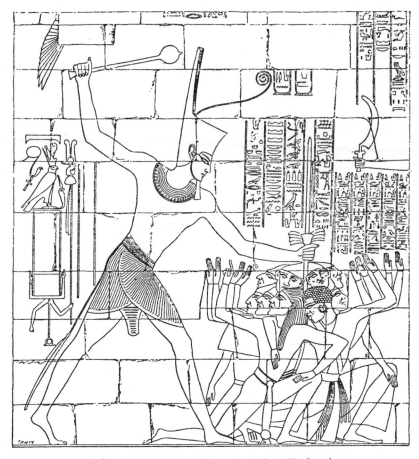

Figure 16. An Egyptian Pharoah Strikes His Captives.

the summer of 588, a strong Egyptian force appeared in the south of Palestine and made threatening gestures against the Babylonians encamped before Jerusalem. Within days the siege of the city was lifted, as the captains of Nebuchadrezzar urged their men toward this new and more pressing danger. They left behind a desolate and ravaged countryside, but also a viable Jerusalem where, for the first time in months, individuals could move freely in and out of the city gates. The city's joys were unbounded, and men and women congratulated one another that their estimate of their God and his power had been right all along. Jerusalem was simply inviolate, and that was the sum of the matter; God had saved his city before, and he would continue to do so. Hadn't the "right" prophets said as much all the while? In fact, many reflected that there had been just too much fuss about the Babylonian threat in the first place, and the best course at the present was to get back to business as usual. And so the sacrificial fires grew cool and the Temple prayers less audible. And upon the king's command the Jewish slaves were taken back into custody and returned to their masters for use in the newly liberated fields. "All's well that ends well," chortled the princely council, and King Zedekiah nodded his assent.

Jeremiah now appeared before the king in a paroxysm of fury (Jer. 34:8–22). In violent language he denounced the treachery of men who, for purposes of expediency, would extinguish the freedom which they had granted their own countrymen and who would violate the oath to God upon which that freedom had been proclaimed. And as for Egypt, she would prove a worthless friend:

> Thus says the LORD, God of Israel: "Thus shall you say to the king of Judah who sent you to me to inquire of me, 'Behold, Pharaoh's army which came to help you is about to return to Egypt, to its own land. And the Chaldeans shall come back and fight against this city; they shall take it and burn it with fire. Thus says the LORD, Do not deceive yourselves, saying, "The Chaldeans will surely stay away from us," for they will not stay away. For even if you should defeat the whole army of Chaldeans who are fighting against you, and there remained of them only wounded men, every man in his tent, they would rise up and burn this city with fire.' "
>
> (Jer. 37:7–10)

Shortly afterward, as Jeremiah left Jerusalem to inquire about his family's welfare following the Babylonian occupation of Anathoth, he was detained at the Benjamin Gate by a sentry who suspected that the prophet was defecting to the Babylonian ranks (Jer. 37:11–15). Despite Jeremiah's denials, he was arrested and, when his enemies at the royal court heard of his detention, they sent their henchmen who flogged the prophet with a whip and pitched him into a dungeon.

Yet the king, whose anxieties had been aroused by Jeremiah's oracle, had the prophet led by a secret entrance into the royal apartments.

"Is there any word from the Lord about me?" inquired the nervous Zedekiah (Jer. 37:16–21).

And Jeremiah, pinioned between his commitment to God and the wounds to his pride and to his person, admitted that there was. "You shall be delivered into the hand of the king of Babylon," he blurted and then, falling to the floor before the king and exposing the open wounds upon his back to the royal gaze, the prophet wept for mercy.

Zedekiah was not a man openly to defy the will of his nobles by granting Jeremiah his freedom, however much he might sympathize with the earnestness of the prophet. But he could at least reduce Jeremiah's suffering. And so he had the prophet confined to new, less harsh surroundings in the quarters of the palace guard.

The hopes which Zedekiah and his advisors set upon the Egyptian relief column were soon shattered, as Jeremiah had promised. By a means yet to be discovered, the Babylonians quickly disposed of Apries' threat to their southern flank and were shortly dug in once more around Jerusalem's walls. And although all demands upon the Jews that they surrender were brusquely dismissed, a quiet despair began to settle in upon the city.

While occasional Jewish patrols probed for weaknesses in the Babylonian lines, the strategy dictated by Nebuchadrezzar from his headquarters at Riblah, in central Syria, was that of a patient reduction of the city by starvation. And as week followed dreary week, sporadic bursts of fighting, often at night, were virtually the only relief to the endless days of waiting and watching. For a time, the popular theology, with its smooth words assuring the perpetuity of Temple and city, was reinvoked and once more the priests were busy with their prayers and their sacrificial fires. But with the passage of the months, even this promise began to wear away, as the city's stores of meat and grain were consumed and horses, dogs, rats, and children were slaughtered for food (Lam. 2:20; 4:10). Through the rainy winter of 588–587 and the soft, fragrant spring which followed, Jerusalem held the enemy at bay only by virtue of her thick stone walls. And all the while, nourishments grew more scarce, as also did hope.

At about this time, word came to Jeremiah in prison that a field in Anathoth belonging to his cousin Hanamel would have to be sold, apparently because the man had been brought to financial grief by the devastation of the Babylonian invasion. Jeremiah agreed to purchase the field in order to retain it within the family, and he commented:

> For thus says the LORD: Just as I have brought all this great evil upon this people, so I will bring upon them all the good that I promise them. Fields shall be bought in this land of which you are saying, It is a desolation . . .
>
> (Jer. 32:42f.)

Meanwhile, the seige ground slowly and monstrously on.

Jeremiah's Final Meeting With Zedekiah

The frigid mud which encased Jeremiah's legs and slithered up the surface of his abdomen was at first a cool if unwelcome relief to the parching heat of the Jerusalem summer (Jer. 38:1–13). But with the pro-

Figure 17. Assyrian Troops Assault a City.

gression of the hours, the mud inserted a gnawing chill into the prophet's body and glazed over the marrow of his soul. Jeremiah's confinement here in the cistern of Malchiah was the ultimate expression of the rage and frustration of his enemies at their own imprisonment within Jerusalem's battlements. Being powerless to strike at the encircling Babylonians who quietly waited for time to accomplish its work, a quartet of royal advisors who had learned to loathe Jeremiah for what seemed to them his treasonous views toward Nebuchadrezzar had asked Zedekiah for the prophet's life.

The king had consented and Jeremiah was led out of his cell in the chambers of the palace guard and thrust into an abandoned well, where his tormentors assumed that he would slowly and agonizingly die of starvation and exposure. Jeremiah himself may well have been as certain of his death in this spot as were his enemies, and all of those anguished cries to God which he had uttered on other occasions, mixed pleas and curses, were now doubtless repeated.

> Why is my pain unceasing,
>   my wound incurable,
>   refusing to be healed?
> Wilt thou be to me like a deceitful brook,
>   like waters that fail?
>   (Jer. 15:18)

But help arrived from an unexpected quarter. An Ethopian eunuch at the royal court, Ebedmelech, hearing of Jeremiah's plight, went to Zedekiah with a request that he be allowed to save the prophet. The king, who by this time was too torn by vacillation and indecision to say no to anyone, extended his permission, and the eunuch, with the help of three lackeys whom the king had made available to him, hoisted Jeremiah out of the well.

Figure 18. Breaching a City Wall. Assyrian Carving.

Zedekiah was now grasping for straws, and he asked that the prophet be brought to the king's private entrance to the Temple courtyard where he might question him secretly (Jer. 38:14–28). Once more the king asked for some hopeful word from God. And once more the prophet, after extracting a promise from the king that he would not again compromise his life, replied that God's only word was that Zedekiah must place himself in the hands of Nebuchadrezzar. Further resistance would mean nothing else than further suffering by Zedekiah himself and by his people.

Once more in prison, Jeremiah spoke again, his voice searching beyond the present death and sounding new dimensions of rebirth and transformation. Jerusalem was, for now, beyond salvation, he gently observed. But there would be a new day in which God would take up a fresh dialogue with his people. And not only would God's people be transformed, but the very nature of the divine discourse would be changed. No longer, as in the days of Moses, would God say, "Do this," or "Don't do that." His very presence would be engraved upon the bosom of his people in such a fashion that their volition, their visceral inclinations would be consonant with his own.

> Behold, the days are coming, says the LORD, when I will make a new covenant with the house of Israel and the house of Judah, not like the covenant which I made with their fathers when I took them by the hand to bring them out of the land of Egypt, my covenant which they broke, though I was their husband, says the LORD. But this is the covenant which I will make with the house of Israel after those days, says the LORD: I will put my law within them, and I will write it upon their hearts; and I will be their God, and they shall be my people. And no longer shall each man teach his neighbor and each his brother, saying, "Know the LORD," for they shall all know me, from the least of them to the greatest, says the LORD; for I will forgive their iniquity, and I will remember their sin no more.

(Jer. 31:31–34)

Jerusalem Falls

Jeremiah had enjoyed his last royal audience. On a sizzling day in July, 587, with Jerusalem's supplies and her will to resist consumed by a year and a half of siege, a Babylonian assault force breached the city wall and poured in upon the terrified inhabitants. No quarter was given and the shrieks of men, women, and children mingled with the frenetic clatter of Babylonian horses and the staccato of Babylonian military commands in a melange of death.

The king and his closest advisors, forseeing the end, had slipped out of the city by night and, picking their way carefully through the Babylonian positions, rode in terror toward the Jordan valley, apparently hoping to find their way to friendly Ammon, where rebels still thumbed their noses at Babylonian might (Jer. 39:1–10; 2 Kings 25:1–12). But they were overtaken by a Babylonian patrol near Jericho and carried in chains to Nebuchadrezzar at Riblah. There Zedekiah was forced to watch the murder of his sons by Babylonian executioners. And to insure that the memory of that grisly scene would remain seared upon his mind, the light of Zedekiah's day was snuffed by Babylonian swordsmen who gouged his eyeballs from their sockets. Still in chains, this pitiful, blinded shell of a man, the last descendant of David to sit upon Judah's throne, was led away to Babylon, there to be confined until his death.

In Jerusalem itself death was joined by other horrors. Thousands of citizens of all stations in life were routed from their homes and, at the prodding of spearpoints, began the long, sorrowful march to Babylon (2 Kings 25:13–21). The city itself, populated now by virtually none save the poorest and most unskilled, was razed. Solomon's magnificent Temple was set in flames, as was the royal palace and other of Jerusalem's larger and more imposing structures. And when the fires had licked up all combustible materials, Babylonian soldiers pulled down the sanctuary's

Figure 19. A King Blinding His Captive. From an Assyrian Representation.

blackened walls and added their rubble to that of the city's defenses which also had been toppled to their foundations.

As a political prisoner, Jeremiah was freed from his cell before the destruction of the palace and was offered asylum in Babylon by Nebuzaradan, the Babylonian military commander (Jer. 39:11–14; 40:1–6). But the prophet, now in the upper reaches of middle life, expressed a desire to remain in his land and among the few Jews left there. And so he was provided with food and money by the Babylonians and set free.

The Murder of Gedeliah

One final, ugly episode was yet to be enacted. Nebuchadrezzar, who had decided that the physical destruction of Jerusalem must be accompanied by her political destruction as well, dissolved the monarchy and, in its stead, appointed a governor over Judah. The man chosen was a member of an influential Jewish family, Gedaliah, whose father Ahikam had intervened to help save Jeremiah's life following the provocative "Temple sermon" in the early days of Jehoiakim's reign (Jer. 26:24). Gedaliah may have been chosen for this task because he was perhaps one of the few individuals of authority in Zedekiah's court with detectable pro-Babylonian inclinations. Due to the vast devastation in Jerusalem, the new governor established his administration in Mizpah, just to the north, and there Jeremiah and handful of other Jewish refugees settled in to build a new life.

But in a last act of rage against Babylon and all who cooperated with her, a fanatic Jew named Ishmael, a cousin of King Zedekiah who had escaped to Ammon, returned and murdered Gedaliah (Jer. 41:1f.). A group of the dead governor's friends, although having no complicity in the crime, nevertheless feared the wrath of the Babylonians. They therefore took Jeremiah as a hostage and fled to the safety of the court of Pharaoh Apries. There we last hear from the prophet of Anathoth, now an old man, forecasting the destruction of Egypt by Nebuchadrezzar. And in Jerusalem jackels prowled the deserted streets and wolves bayed at the cold, unblinking moon, while a solitary voice softly chanted:

> Women are ravished in Zion,
>   virgins in the towns of Judah.
> Princes are hung up by their hands;
>   no respect is shown to the elders.
> Young men are compelled to grind at the mill;
>   and boys stagger under loads of wood.
> The old men have quit the city gate,
>   the young men their music.
> The joy of our hearts has ceased;
>   our dancing has been turned to mourning.
>   (Lam. 5:11–15)

III.

EXILE

(587–538 B.C.)

By the waters of Babylon,
there we sat down and wept,
when we remembered Zion.
On the willows there
we hung up our lyres.
For there our captors
required of us songs,
and our tormentors, mirth, saying,
"Sing us one of the songs of Zion!"

How shall we sing the LORD's *song*
in a foreign land?
If I forget you, O Jerusalem,
let my right hand wither!
Let my tongue cleave to the roof
of my mouth,
if I do not remember you,
if I do not set Jerusalem
above my highest joy!
                    —Psalm 137:1–6

Chapter Four

*Then he said to me, "The guilt of the house of Israel and
Judah is exceedingly great; the land is full of blood, and
the city full of injustice; for they say, 'The* LORD *has for-
saken the land, and the* LORD *does not see.' As for me, my
eye will not spare, nor will I have pity, but I will requite
their deeds upon their heads."*

—*Ezekiel 9:9f.*

Life in Exile[14]

Poor, blinded Zedekiah presented a pathetic spectacle as he was paraded down Babylon's broad, palm-shaded Processional Way, the grand
avenue which coursed its splendid path from the Ishtar Gate southward
into the heart of the imperial city. We may imagine that the last king of
Judah was manacled, and the wide leather collar tightly embracing his
neck was festooned by an iron chain which provided a leash to the
grinning Babylonian cavalry officer who led the monarch along. Behind
the king, in frightened, knotted groups, trailed thousands of his subjects,
terrified men, women, and children struggling along between a double
file of Babylonian swordsmen. A few of the men wore the shredded remains of military uniforms, but most of the captives were clothed in
soiled and tattered smocks of the simplest manufacture. Some carried
small, cloth-bound balls of food or possessions. Others held hands in an
effort to probe for some tangible comfort to soothe their weariness and
fear.

Along the Way, clusters of Babylonian citizens had assembled, many
of them children, and the sound of their laughter and jeers lifted with the
dust raised by the shuffling feet of this huge centipede. Figs, dates, and
rotten pomegranates etched trajectories through the sun-drenched air,
soft missiles aimed at Hebrew heads. Zedekiah, whose blindness rendered
him particularly vulnerable, was a favorite target, and long before he
reached the steps of the royal palace, the juice of a hundred fruits dripped
from his face and body, while insects, attracted by this sweet pungency,
swarmed thirstily about his head.

In the great hall of the palace, Nebuchadrezzar's chair of state stood
vacant, the king being yet in Syria preparing for the assault upon Tyre.
Down below in less sumptuous surroundings, royal stewards prepared a
cell for the Judean king, while not far away, another son of David, the

still young Jehoiachin, heard the noise outside and, guessing its meaning, wept as the memories of another such procession of ten years before stabbed at his brain.

This second group of Judean exiles who wearily trooped into Babylon in 587 had at least some idea of the type of treatment with which they would be greeted and, although they hardly welcomed it, it was at least susceptible of comprehension. No such knowledge, however, had softened the terror of the first wave of captives of a decade before who, with their boy king, had been forced over the blistering sands from Jerusalem to Babylon following the first capitulation of their city. Their arrival in Nebuchadrezzar's capital in the late spring of 597 was accompanied by all of their most grotesque anxieties concerning their fate, grim visions which ranged from permanent physical imprisonment to death by torture. But as events unfolded, it soon became apparent that the very worst possibilities, at least, would be avoided. Some few were impressed into various forms of manual service by the Babylonian government; but most were settled, by family unit, outside the walls of Babylon onto land which had been newly irrigated as a part of Nebuchadrezzar's scheme of public works. There they were set to work claiming this soil for agriculture and raising crops with which to feed Babylon's burgeoning population. Only the members of the royal family and the king's closest advisors suffered actual incarceration.

If any among this first group of Jewish exiles was delighted at Nebuchadrezzar's sufferance, however, that delight rapidly evaporated in the searing Mesopotamian heat. Few of the exiles were accustomed to such conditions of climate and labor. They had been the merchants, the intellectuals, the priests, and the aristocrats of a proud City of David. Their bodies, habituated to a higher elevation with its frequent frosts in winter and the cooling breezes of its summer evenings, sweltered in the broiling Euphrates valley where the progression of the seasons is virtually unknown. And their hands, which had counted out money or pushed ink pens over smooth parchment scrolls, cracked and bled when harnessing Babylonian oxen and guiding Babylonian plows. Longingly they remembered Jerusalem, recalled the sweetness of their lives in that sacred city, and wondered about their kinsmen still there. Some were tempted to escape, for Babylonian security around the Jewish enclosures was extremely light and guards could be easily avoided at night. But where then would they go? The hundreds of miles to Jerusalem were all under Babylonian control, and even the city itself was presided over by a Babylonian garrison. Therefore, since capture meant death, the exiles grudgingly performed their painful tasks and waited for news from home.

What they heard was not calculated to inspire hope. The new king, Zedekiah, had been enthroned amid the singing of chants and psalms as

Figure 20. Man Driving Animals. Assyrian Bronze.

old as the dynasty of David itself. And he had gathered a new cadre of courtiers and advisors to replace those who were now in exile. And as the old aristocrats lost their titles to the new, so virtually all of the exiles were relieved of their land. With the exception of small householders, many of whom were not touched by the first deportation of 597, a large share of the landowners of Judah, especially the proprietors of the great estates, now found themselves forcibly resettled in this distant place and their properties claimed by their kinsmen at home. "They have gone far from the Lord," agreed Zedekiah's nobles, "to us this land is given as a possession" (Ezek. 11:15). The message thus borne by the hot winds off the desert was that Jerusalem no longer expected the exiles to return and that, even if they did, they would be unwelcome intruders upon a society which had already forgotten them.

The jibe voiced by the people in Judah also pointed to another dimension of the crisis which now descended upon the exiles: the loss of their land and their deportation to this alien and inhospitable terrain implied the loss of their identity as Jews and their forfeiture of the spiritual traditions of Abraham, Moses, and David. The God of Israel, who was supposed to shape nations and events, now seemed puny and remote, a Deity holed up in the far-off Jerusalem Temple who was either unable or unwilling to blunt the sword of Nebuchadrezzar and save His own people. Did not the victory of the Babylonians and the humiliation of the Lord's own people signal the superiority of Marduk and the rest of the Babylonian pantheon? Or—even worse—did not the exiles' calamitous experience and their disinheritance by their own more fortunate compatriots spell the death of *all* sensible theology, the extinguishing of the last glowing ember that faith and life have any connection whatsoever?

As their plows furrowed the rich alluvial silt of the Mesopotamian valley, the Jews of the exile probed their bruised souls for the solutions to these riddles, and their anguished community began to exhibit the divergent answers which they found there. Some capitulated to the Babylonian theology and joined their captors in their worship and prayers. Others submerged into a denial of self and a denial of hope and, turning their backs upon ultimate meanings altogether, resignedly worked their oxen, fed their bellies, and grew old. But most stood suspended between hope and despair, not wanting to give up the old formulas of faith, yet neither able to derive meaning or succor from them.

It was into this vacuum of the spirit that Ahab ben Kolaiah and Zedekiah ben Maaseiah were sucked. If no meaning could be found in the exiles' present plight, perhaps one could be forced upon it. And so, presenting themselves as spokesmen of God, they uttered incantations of revolt. Babylon would die, smitten by the God of Israel, they furtively prophesied. Or God would bend Nebuchadrezzar's heart, as in the days of Moses he had bent Pharaoh's heart, into setting the captives free. But Babylonian ears were sharp to such corrosive words and Babylonian hands soon lashed the prophets to the stake. The crackle of the burning tender did not drown their death-screams, nor did the thick, acrid smoke, curling upward, obliterate the sight of the terror on their faces (Jer. 29:20–23). And their charred corpses suggested strongly to the exiles who silently watched their incineration that God was about to do no such thing. The letter from Jeremiah which arrived in Babylon before the memory of this gruesome scene had grown cold, advising the exiles to settle in for a long life of alienation from their homeland, was protested by some among the Babylonian Jews (Jer. 29:4–9). But others remem-

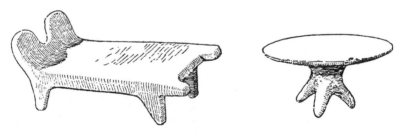

Figure 21. Earthen Bed and Table from Babylon.

bered his earlier warnings and worried that this forecast would also prove true. And when King Zedekiah, following his seditious meeting in Jerusalem with the ambassadors of Tyre, Sidon, Edom, Moab, and Ammon, was summoned to Babylon to account for himself before Nebuchadrezzar, the exiles began to comprehend that they would not soon see their homes again—if ever!

Ezekiel's First Oracles[15]

Among the exiles was a young man of an especially sensitive and receptive spirit. The son of a priest, he had been born in 622, the year before the dramatic presentation to King Josiah of the scroll of the Book of the Law. His earliest years had therefore coincided with the Great Reformation and, as he learned his letters at the Temple school, he also learned a deep and abiding love for the God who had chosen that place as His sanctuary and for the forms of worship practiced there. His admiring eyes bathed themselves in the liquid colors of the priestly vestments, and his nostrils reveled in the aromas of incense and of smoke from the sacrificial fires. The very blocks of the building were for him a most desired species of precious stone.

His adolescence straddled those years between the death of King Josiah and the first surrender of the city to the Babylonians in 597 and, as the ideals of the Great Reformation rapidly dissolved to be replaced by their cheap counterfeit, the young man found himself taking instruction from those who struggled to preserve the integrity of Temple worship and to resist the reimposition of pagan shrines and prayers. It was not a happy battle, and those who waged it felt the momentum slipping from their grasp. To be sure, there were infrequent bursts of liturgical energy, occasions when the Temple pulsed with tramping feet of worshipping multitudes and purred with the chants of a thousand prayers, as on the day when the Babylonian army, flushed with its victory at Carchemish, first bore down upon the city. But perceptive men and women knew the shallowness of such retreats, even if they had not had Jeremiah or the scribe Baruch there to point it out to them.

The young man was himself a fledgling priest, just turned twenty five, when his even tenderer contemporary Jehoiachin inherited a throne and a hopeless rebellion from his newly dead father. The fall of the city and the looting of the Temple of its treasures were blows to the *solar plexus* of his soul, and when he was selected from the Temple rolls by the Babylonian military to join the long column of men, women, and children to be marched off with the king into captivity, he very nearly wished for death.

For five years now Ezekiel had lived with his fellow expatriots on a farm at Tel-abib near the Chebar Canal, a main arterial waterway a few miles south of Babylon (Ezek. 3:15). In those years he had suffered the deprivations of home and Temple more than most of the exiles, for his pensive and reflective nature rendered him highly susceptible to such anguish. And the questions of faith and destiny which troubled his fellow deportees pressed with unusual sharpness upon his heart. He was given to frequent dreams which, occuring at first only at night, soon imposed themselves upon his waking hours as well. Initially, these were clearly recognizable memories, the effort of a bruised and troubled brain to compensate for present anguish by recapturing the joy of the past. And in such experiences Ezekiel was once more at home in the Temple, among the tutors and the other aspirants to the priesthood with whom he had spent so many happy hours.

But, with the passage of time, the shape and venue of the visions changed. Although richly impregnated with the symbols of the past, they no longer recalled his yesterdays, but in a wordless and inchoate fashion began to take the shape of the present. The easy hopes raised by Ahab ben Kolaiah and Zedekiah ben Maaseiah were now as charred as their bodies, and King Zedekiah had returned from his audience with Nebuchadrezzar, tail between his legs. With ferocious urgency the questions which had simmered in the captives' brains began to boil. And Ezekiel was devastated by God.

> As I looked, behold, a stormy wind came out of the north, and a great cloud, with brightness round about it, and fire flashing forth continually, and in the midst of the fire, as it were gleaming bronze. And from the midst of it came the likeness of four living creatures. And this was their appearance: they had the form of men, but each had four faces, and each of them had four wings.
>
> Now as I looked at the living creatures, I saw a wheel upon the earth beside the living creatures, one for each of the four of them. As for the appearance of the wheels and their construction: their appearance was like the gleaming of a chrysolite; and the four had the same likeness, their construction being as it were a wheel within a wheel.
>
> Such was the appearance of the likeness of the glory of the LORD. And when I saw it, I fell upon my face, and I heard the voice of one speaking. And he said to me, "Son of man, stand upon your feet, and I will speak with you. . . . I send you to the people Israel. . . . And whether they hear or refuse to hear (for they are a rebellious house) they will know that there has been a prophet among them.
>
> (Ezek. 1:4–2:5 *passim*)

A sense of liberation passed over Ezekiel and energized the most intimate synapses of his soul. The very "glory of the Lord," that term by which the Temple priests had spoken of the here-and-nowness of a Deity who overarched and transcended all human categories, was *here*, in Babylon, among the exiles. God himself had words to speak and he, Ezekiel, would be the bearer of those words.

> And he said to me, "Son of man, eat what is offered to you; eat this scroll, and go, speak to the house of Israel." So I opened my mouth, and he gave me the scroll to eat. And he said to me, "Son of man, eat this scroll that I give you and fill your stomach with it." Then I ate it; and it was in my mouth as sweet as honey.
>
> (Ezek. 3:1–3)

Ezekiel Prophesies Judgment Upon Jerusalem

The year by modern reckoning designated 592 B.C. gave way to its successor. In Babylon the court historians, having impressed upon clay their brief account of the events of Nebuchadrezzar's twelfth and thirteenth regnal years, decided that the facilities of the royal archives were becoming cramped and that another repository would have to be found for this and subsequent slabs of the Babylonian Chronicle. It was a decision which would deny to future archaeologists important discoveries and to future generations an instructive slice of the history of the New Babylonian Empire.

Also in Babylon, the grinding of time's wheel had begun to effect certain changes upon the community of Jewish exiles. Many of the more senior deportees of 597 and others who, although not old in years, had surrendered their spirits to this harsh and rootless life expired and were laid in the warm Babylonian soil under ancient Hebrew prayers for the dead. At the other end of the spectrum of life, a gaggle of Hebrew children, who had never known or couldn't remember Jerusalem, played in the village streets, splashed in the warm canals, and painstakingly formed their *alephs* and *beths* under the watchful eyes of Hebrew masters.

Their elders strained for snatches of information from far-off Jerusalem and pounced upon each fragment of news over the king's growing intransigence and the scornful oracles of Jeremiah. But what fascinated and dismayed them the most were the condescending slurs which continued to be cast in their direction by the Jerusalem Jews. As the smooth self-certainty of the pro-Egyptian party at Zedekiah's court grew measurably with the passing months, each communication from the exiles was met in official circles by, first, indifference, then virtual repudiation. "The diseased branches have been lopped away; let the healthy vine now bear its good fruit," became a philosophy to be heard with increasing frequency, especially from circles near the Crown (cf. Ezek. 15:1–8). And if Jeremiah decried such vapid foolishness and if individual loved ones in

Jerusalem sent contrary assurances to the exiles, the wounds to the self-identity of the captives were nonetheless deep and crippling (Jer. 24).

The priest Ezekiel was now attracting a certain attention to himself by his words and by his odd behavior. The pressure of the exile had pushed not a few persons into eccentricity and even insanity. But the bizarre of Ezekiel's deeds was singular because of the words by which he fashioned an interpretative commentary to it. On one warm spring morning Ezekiel had sat in the street near his home and, as his Jewish neighbors looked on in wonder and in amusement, had shaved his head and beard, carefully piling the clippings upon a scale. After weighing the shorn mass into three equal quantities, he burned one handful in the street, hacked away at the second with a borrowed sword, and, walking around, tossed the third by increments into the air. Then he solemnly intoned,

> Thus says the Lord GOD: This is Jerusalem. . . . A third part of you shall die of pestilence and be consumed with famine in the midst of you; a third part of you shall fall by the sword round about you; and a third part I will scatter to all the winds and will unsheathe the sword after them.
>
> (Ezek. 5:5, 12)

Shortly after that strange day, Ezekiel confided to a group of astonished priests who were in his home that, in a vision, the Lord had carried him to Jerusalem (Ezek. 8:1–11:13). There he had been shown an outrageous variety of vulgar rituals displayed in the Temple—the drawing of magic and salacious pictures on the Temple walls, the veneration of imported gods, the adoration of the sun—and that upon the initiative of the Lord he had told those who practiced such horrors that they would die by the swords of foreigners like those whose ridiculous worship they aped. So vivid was the event that, even as Ezekiel spoke to these Jerusalem Jews, one of them, Pelatiah the son of Benaiah, fell dead.

Eyebrows were cocked at yet another instance of Ezekiel's heterodox speech and movement. Being asked to deliver the homily at an informal service of worship, the only form of corporate devotion available to the Temple-less deportees, Ezekiel began a recital of Israel's history before God (Ezek. 20). It was an established rubric, one whose origins harked back to the patriarchs of old and which had become especially popular in certain Jewish quarters from the time of Josiah's Reformation (cf. Deut. 6:20f., 26:5–9; Josh. 24:2–13). But as the story of Israel's life began to pour off the tongue of Ezekiel, the worshippers heard no grand recital of covenant solidarity between God and his people. Their tingling ears listened as, instead, Ezekiel narrated a tale of God's continued love and of Israel's persistent refusal to accept that love. The haunted priest insisted that, as long ago as the exodus from Egypt, an epoch praised by Jews as an unusually fruitful time in their relationship with God, Israel had stubbornly resisted God's overtures and had returned his mercy with spite and neglect. In the shocked silence which followed this unusual translation of Israel's ancient creed, Ezekiel announced that Jerusalem would be destroyed.

Yet this novel priest had still another electrifying way of conceptualizing Israel's standing before God, a parable of sex and depravity.

> The word of the LORD came to me: "Son of man, there were two women, the daughters of one mother; they played the harlot in Egypt; they played the harlot in their youth; there their breasts were pressed and their virgin bosoms handled. Oholah was the name of the elder and Oholibah the name of her sister. They became mine, and they bore sons and daughters. As for their names, Oholah is Samaria [i.e., the Northern Kingdom], and Oholibah is Jerusalem.

> "Oholah played the harlot while she was mine; and she doted on her lovers the Assyrians, warriors clothed in purple, governors and commanders, all of them desirable young men. . . . Therefore I delivered her into the hands of her lovers, into the hands of the Assyrians, upon whom she doted. These uncovered her nakedness; they seized her sons and her daughters; and her they slew with the sword. . . .

> "Her sister Oholibah saw this, yet she was more corrupt than she in her doting and in her harlotry, which was worse than that of her sister. . . . And the Babylonians came to her into the bed of love, and they defiled her with their lust. . . ."

> Therefore, O Oholibah, thus says the Lord GOD: "Behold, I will rouse against you your lovers. . . . And they shall come against you from the north with chariots and wagons and a host of peoples; they shall set themselves against you on every side with buckler, shield, and helmet, and I will commit the judgment to them, and they shall judge you according to their judgments."

> (Ezek. 23:1–24, *passim*)

If the image of God's choosing to marry two harlots seemed blasphemous to some, so be it. The real blasphemy, contended Ezekiel, resided in the soul of the people. They were rotten and fraudulent when God chose them, and all of his mercy and grace had been unable to alter that salient fact. Thus, as God had destroyed Samaria, so he would destroy Jerusalem.

The impact which Ezekiel's unusual declarations had upon the exiled community began to run deep. And it was not without a certain ambiguity. To one side, the specter of a further devastation upon Jerusalem shot chills of apprehension and terror into their souls. These captives knew better than anyone else the full horror which such a calamity implied. And as they compared the reports of Zedekiah's belligerent posturings with the slicing, if cryptic, analyses by Ezekiel, fortified by similar prognoses from Jeremiah, their fears mounted that a new clash of arms was imminent from which Judah would earn nothing but decimation. When that moment arrived, their continued presence in this hostile and alien land was assured.

But beyond gloom, Ezekiel's words began to coax the first blush of what was almost, but not quite, a hope. For the priest-prophet was painting for them a surrealistic, yet vivid portrait of the essential unity of God's people before the Almighty and was, at the same sitting, etching onto the canvas of their lives a coherent reasonableness concerning what had happened to them and what seemed to be about to happen to their friends and relatives at home. God's people had failed to reply in trust to his gracious and compassionate overtures, not once, but repeatedly and dogmatically over the long years of their relationship. And now, in a cul-de-sac formed by their own intransigence and foolishness, they had suffered the pangs of that anguish which the Northern Kingdom had endured before them and which the rest of Jerusalem's family would shortly undergo. Yet even here in Babylon God was present among his people in his "glory." And that being true, the forceful implication was that God had yet fresh chapters to write in the saga of his people.

Ezekiel, however, wished to go beyond implication and to erect concrete avowals that the exiles were cut off neither from their land nor from their God. And in doing so he orchestrated a théme of spiritual transformation and internal renewal, an intended counterpoint, perhaps, to Jeremiah's strikingly similar melody:

> Thus says the Lord GOD: I will gather you from the peoples, and assemble you out of the countries where you have been scattered, and I will give you the land of Israel. . . . And I will give them one heart, and put a new spirit within them; I will take the stony heart out of their flesh and give them a heart of flesh, that they may walk in my statutes and keep my ordinances and obey them; and they shall be my people, and I will be their God.
>
> (Ezek. 11:17–20; cf. Jer. 31:31f.)

Exile Greets Exile

When the news arrived in Babylon that King Zedekiah had ordered the successful assault upon the Babylonian garrison in Jerusalem and that all Judah was aflame with revolt, the exiled community feared reprisal. The memory of the abortive uprising under Ahab ben Kolaiah and Zedekiah ben Maaseiah and its horrifying aftermath were fresh enough in both Jewish and Babylonian memories for each community to take certain steps toward self-protection. As for the captors, the fear of a Jewish riot in Babylon caused an intensification of security within the Jewish enclaves and a heightened presence there of armed military patrols, while from the captives there issued repeated protestations of peace. We may suppose that a few young Jewish firebrands did meet secretly to see what could be done to help the combatants at home, but having decided that they were impotent to intervene, they offered prayers for Zedekiah's health and went back to work.

By February of 588 the first wave of Nebuchadrezzar's assault force had surrounded the city and, for the eighteen months which followed, as Jerusalem was slowly starved into submission, the exiles remained largely ignorant of events within the city. Occasional military communiques to the capital leaked into Jewish ears, and certain of the exiles, having served their masters as interpreters in the field, returned to Babylon with fragments of information about the welfare of the city. But as this battle of attrition offered few prisoners of war, specific data about the fortunes of friends and family were deprived the exiles. And when, in the late summer of 587, the news arrived that Jerusalem had capitulated, the response of the Babylonian Jews was one of pained relief, Ezekiel prominently insisting that no tears should be shed for the fallen city (Ezek. 24:15–27). Then, as the initial wave of Zedekiah's subdued rebels arrived in Babylon, gaunt, terrified, and exhausted, they were eagerly met and hungrily interrogated by the older exiles.

These were days in which joy and sorrow were almost indistinguishable from one another. Zedekiah's fellow insurgents, trooping into the city, betrayed the anxiety of newly caged game about to grace the spit of the trapper. And scarcely less gloomy over Jerusalem's new disgrace and violent destruction were the senior exiles among whom all hope of a return to the City of David lay bleeding and torn. But the grief of the moment was brushed aside as fathers and sons, brothers and sisters, separated for a decade, embraced and wept. And if old jealousies and enmities were also resumed, even they pealed with a certain joy.

The exiles of 587 shifted their weight to share their broken lives with this new flood of deportees. Out in the country the artisans of a decade before, now turned plowmen, lectured the new arrivals on the temperament of Babylonian oxen and schooled them in the mechanics of a sluice gate. And in the villages, where Jews lived side to side with exiled Damascenes, Assyrians, Moabites, and Cretans, the new captives practiced their ancient domestic and commercial arts and mastered new ones.

The men and women of the second deportation learned from the senior exiles in other ways, as well. Although a handful of the older captives had tried, with varying degrees of success, to integrate themselves

Figure 22. Artist's Conception of a Babylonian Street Scene.

into the tissue of Babylonian life—sporting Babylonian clothing, brandishing Babylonian speech, worshipping Babylonian gods, applying for Babylonian jobs—the exiled community as a whole had opted for their continued Jewishness. The priests might have no Temple, but they could yet lead the people in hymns and prayers to the God of Israel and, on occasion, devise new forms of devotion and petition. The spiritual crisis called forth by the disaster of 597 had spurred the search for liturgical innovation and thus new rituals, or more precisely, fresh variations upon the old, greeted and surprised the recent arrivals.

The royal person of young King Jehoiachin might languish in a perfumed cell, as might those of his ministers in less pleasant confinements, but much of the petty bureaucracy of the old times moved freely among the exiles, and around them, the "elders of Judah," there grew up structures for the administration and adjudication of minor affairs. If such an arrangement lacked the stamp of Davidic authority, that need was supplied by the simple recognition among his exiled subjects that Jehoiachin was yet their *de jure* king, and the new structures certainly boasted a democratic and popular bias such as Judah had not known since distant pre-monarchial days.

Although the larger Jewish family might now be sundered into its Babylonian and Jerusalemite components, the smaller unit of father, mother, and child was retained. And not just retained, but propagated by the fecund marriage of maturing young exiles and the creation of new familial lines even here in captivity. Jeremiah's urgings to this end were doubtless of influence in leading some of the Babylonian Jews to undertake the vows of marriage, and the lesson of the eradication in Assyrian captivity of the family solidarity and, ultimately, of the very identity of the Hebrews of the Northern Kingdom a century before had a like effect. Thus the newer exiles, who only shortly before had appropriated the property and the pride of their captive cousins, now began with gratitude to fit themselves as best they could into patterns of life which those cousins had erected in this uncongenial land.

Meanwhile, back in Riblah, in Syria, Nebuchadrezzar dispatched the main body of his army, now rested from the siege of Jerusalem and enriched by its plunder, to deal with Tyre, while a smaller strike force set out to fall upon Ammon. Speaking to the exiles, Ezekiel declared that these steps were of a choreography written and directed by God:

> For thus says the Lord God: Behold, I will bring upon Tyre from the north Nebuchadrezzar king of Babylon, king of kings, with horses and chariots, and with horsemen and a host of many soldiers. . . . He will set up a seige wall against you, and throw up a mound against you, and raise a roof of shields against you. . . . They will break down your walls and

destroy your pleasant houses; your stones and timber and soil they will cast into the midst of the waters.

(Ezek. 26:7f.)

Life Returns to Jerusalem

Nebuchadrezzar, poring over charts of Phoenicia and thrashing out with his generals a strategy for Tyre, made a quick and all too logical judgment about the Jews. Informed of the murder of his Judean governor, Gedaliah, he snapped his fingers, gestured emphatically with his hands and arms, shouted snatches like "irascible" and "ungovernable," and turned over the whole affair to his administrator for Syria-Palestine. The monarch's contemptuous dismissal of the problem of Judah is understandable, both from the standpoint of the region's history of fractiousness as a Babylonian colony and because the devastation of 587 left little of Judah to fuss over. But the practical effect of Nebuchadrezzar's exasperation was to place Jerusalem under the first non-Hebrew executive she had known since David wrestled the city from the Jebusites more than four centuries earlier.

From Mizpah, where Gedaliah's ill-starred administration had sat for less than a year, a trickle of Jews passed hesitantly along the road to Jerusalem. The secretaries and bureaucrats who had not fled in panic to Egypt after the assassination of their chief had, most of them, decided to return to the city. In spite of the devastation there, many of them owned land and, once it became clear that the Babylonians would not name Gedaliah's successor, they chose to return to it in order to live upon it, if possible. Their motivation was partly economic, for in such distressed times possession was nine points of the law, and their vacant properties, such as they were, could easily be appropriated by intruders unless they themselves were physically present. But the small migration was largely a matter of sentiment and conviction, that ancient affection of the Jew for the very dust of Jerusalem's streets. These men represented the last flayed remains of Judah's body of civil servants still in the land. As their fathers had served good King Josiah, they were even yet the lieutenants of melancholy King Jehoiachin, pining away in his Babylonian prison, the custodians of the royal presence and the royal archives. And if Mizpah was no longer to be a seat of government, then they and their documents would be in Jerusalem, ever the locus of the dynasty of David.

Their initial sight of the city was as a cup of sea water to a thirsty man, lovely yet empoisoned. And it would be difficult to judge who, at that moment, suffered more—those in Babylon who longed for Jerusalem but could not see her, or those at home who saw the city's misery and felt it as their own. Yet there was work to be done and it was quickly undertaken by the returning former officials, not simply for its own necessary sake, but also for the therapeutic balm with which work salves the soul.

A few of the city's houses had escaped destruction and some of these were inhabited by the handful of indigent families whom the Babylonians had considered too insignificant to carry away. Into other such dwellings the former royal scribes and ministers moved with their families, in some cases permanently, in others only until their own damaged homes could be restored. There was no money with which to hire labor, and none but the most rudimentary tools were at hand; but building materials were profuse in the abundant rubble and, as most of it was unclaimed by its distant owners, it could be had for the taking. Also, because the destructive wrath of the Babylonians had been generally confined to the city proper and to other urban strongholds such as Lachish and Azekah, the rural stretches with their pleasant farmlands were yet productive of food which could be obtained at fresh air market through swapping and barter.

Quite slowly then, but with visible deliberation, Jerusalem knotted some of her broken threads. She was yet a tatty garment by anyone's standards; the architectural repairs were amateurish and often makeshift, deserted streets echoed the barks of prowling dogs, and the ubiquitous rubble—piles and piles of rubble—was never out of sight nor out of mind. But still the city functioned, in a primitive and awkward fashion, and her ugly defacement siphoned little of the affection of those few tough Jews who lived there. It is not surprising that those who had served Gedaliah at Mizpah, and Zedekiah and Jehoiachin before that, assumed the leadership of this tiny community. With the exception of a sprinkling of priests left by the Babylonians in the smouldering city, they alone represented the city's literate contact with her structures of history and tradition. Only they and the few available priests knew and could interpret Jerusalem's laws, recite Jerusalem's past, lead Jerusalem's prayers, and school Jerusalem's children. And, with no formalities at all, these things they began to do.

The Temple was now an insane and vulgar heap of debris, but the courtyard nonetheless became a place of outdoor worship where the old creeds were ritually lifted by priests and people and where the ancient prayers were fervently hymned. The altar of burnt offering still stood, its stones blackened as never before by a fire its builders never entertained, and there was some talk of its use in the liturgy. But it was eventually decided that it had been cultically profaned by the events of terrible memory, and no flames were permitted to lick bloodied lambs nor to jab at the bright air above. And so priests and people soon grew accustomed to worship without sacrifice, dreaming all the while of the day when it would be restored.

The remains of the royal palace languished nearby and the soft fingers of former royal scribes were, before long, combing through the massive boulders and the carbon encrusted beams in the search for parchments and scrolls from the archives. Only a few were found to have survived the conflagration, but these were respectfully removed and deposited with great gentleness in a library, previously the home of an official of state, where other royal records and accounts, carted to Mizpah and back again, also reposed. The Babylonians were quite content that all of this should transpire. It did no one harm, and they were much too occupied around Tyre to be bothered by trifles such as this. So an occasional Babylonian cavalry column clattered noisily through what had once been the Ephraim Gate, looked gloweringly around the town, and then rode ostentatiously away.

The "Great History" Is Revised

In periods of anguish the human perception of time is often severely contorted, days assuming the properties of months and years those of days, so that the effort to measure and chronicle time is often neglected as an impossible, or at least fruitless, enterprise. This is especially true if all of those pegs upon which a people is accustomed to hook its experiences—the coronation and death of kings, the sallying forth to war, the visitation of famine or plague—are sheared away. Then life becomes static and stony, a ship becalmed on a currentless ocean, a window glazed into opacity by morning frost. Not that life *is* suspended under those conditions; only that it seems so and that the clocks of the brain tick more and more feebly until they tick no more. Then men cease to calculate and to narrate their own years and they shift to the past their deep-set hunger to systematize human experience. In both Babylon and Jerusalem the Jewish communities, stupefied by the enormity of the destruction of Jerusalem and by the desecration of their holy institutions of Temple cult and Davidic crown, lapse into a continuum of life which, for them, has little chronology. Here in the political and social backwaters of international events, few whirls and eddies relieve the essential tedium of life, or its harshness. And apart from remembering that the captivity of good King Jehoiachin (and thus their own) is now in its twelfth year, or its twentieth, or its twenty-fifth, they scarcely bother to observe if the sands of time still run at all.

They do, however, look behind themselves with renewed and acid-scarred wonder. If there is no need to catalogue an empty present, they fall all the more earnestly upon a tragically pregnant past. Jeremiah's declarations, for so long scorned, have now begun to inject a rationale into the searing desolation of their lives. And Ezekiel, relying upon his predecessors in the prophetic discipline, can be heard reciting a view of Israel's life which graphically limns the profile of the nation's fundamental sinfulness. Yet if Judah is now in chains because she prostituted herself before God, as both Jeremiah and Ezekiel have insisted, how could that fundamental waywardness be related to her identity as a people, to those traditions and institutions which she celebrated as the focus of that identity, and to the God whose endowment that identity was assumed to be? Should not Israel's story, with its plenitude of detail, now be reexamined with a view to shaping it according to those patterns for which the prophets' words and the very agony of the nation cried out? And so the Great History, written in the full flush of Josiah's Reformation, comes to be revised in the light of the nation's subsequent hideous experience.

The enterprise was taken up primarily in Jerusalem, for the documents necessary to such a project, most notably the Great History itself, were there, housed in what remained of the royal archives. And the ideological heirs of the Josianic historians were also there among the remnants of Gedaliah's coterie of scribes and secretaries. It was a vast and fundamental undertaking, and many years and a variety of scribal hands were to move across its pages before it was to reach a tentative and cautious conclusion. That the Jerusalem writers enjoyed the collaboration of some, at least, of their colleagues in Babylon was insured by the efficiency of Nebuchadrezzar's mails.

The second edition of the Great History was concerned, in part, to move beyond the moral graphs and charts which, although appearing quite neat and logical during Josiah's lifetime, had been betrayed by subsequent events as inadequate, even simplistic. It was no longer tenable to hold, as the Great History had done, that the fortunes of war and politics formed a reflex to the piety of the people of God: that when Israel worshipped and behaved correctly all went well, and that when she did not she suffered. Nor could it be boasted, as had the historians of Josiah's day, that during the long years of the nation's division between North and South, that the Judeans had attained a superior piety. The hard, visceral truth was that all Israel, North and South, had betrayed the compassionate overtures of God from the very moment of her election and that now, by means of the nation's devastation and exile, God's grief and anger were lashing forth. The Northern Kingdom had been annihilated and Judah nearly so; perhaps the end of God's loving experiment with his people had come, or perhaps their iniquity was being purged for a new tomorrow. The historians ventured no specific judgment about the future, they only described the past. And upon the rhythmic undulation of good and evil, of prosperity and suffering by

which the Josianic historians had described Israel's past, the historians of
the disaster, without erasing their predecessors' work, superimposed their
own radical vision of sin and judgment, as in their rendering of Joshua's
address to the tribes assembled at Shechem:

> "Now therefore fear the LORD, and serve him in sincerity and in faith-
> fulness; put away the gods which your fathers served beyond the River,
> and in Egypt, and serve the LORD. And if you be unwilling to serve the
> LORD, choose this day whom you will serve, whether the gods your fathers
> served in the region beyond the River, or the gods of the Amorites in
> whose land you dwell; but as for me and my house, we will serve the
> LORD."
>
> Then the people answered, "Far be it from us that we should forsake
> the LORD, to serve other gods; for it is the LORD our God who brought
> us and our fathers up from the land of Egypt, out of the house of bondage,
> and who did those great signs in our sight, and preserved us in all the
> way that we went, and among all the peoples through whom we passed;
> and the LORD drove out before us all the peoples, the Amorites who lived
> in the land; therefore we also will serve the LORD, for he is our God."
>
> But Joshua said to the people, *"You cannot serve the* LORD; *for he is
> a holy God; he is a jealous God; he will not forgive your transgressions
> or your sins."*
>
> (Josh. 24:14–19)

Yet the historians of the calamity were not without hope, as strongly
as such words might suggest that they were. The writing of history itself
implied that someone would read that history and would learn, both
conceptually and spiritually, from it. And Judah's king still reigned, if
only from the cramped confinement of his penal apartment in Nebuchadrezzar's palace. Thus the second edition of the Great History, by insisting upon the absolute rightness and justice of God's deeds even in the
calamity of destruction and exile, urged the tormented nation to accept
the verdict which their Deity had rendered and, in this remarkable fashion, to profess their utter need for and dependence upon him. Then,
perhaps in ways which yet defied the imagination, God might assume
fresh initiatives in their lives.

Ezekiel Speaks of Hope

In Babylon the years which followed the final collapse of Jerusalem
and the second and more massive deportation of her peoples produced a
subtle but profound shift in the thinking of Ezekiel and in his oracles.
The judgment of God, which he both feared and welcomed, had fallen.
Jerusalem was in ruins; Israel's sinfulness had run its ultimate and tragic
course; the holiness of God was affirmed. But the Lord now had in mind
a new course for his people. First, however, the old concepts must be

Figure 23. Enamelled Facade from Nebuchadrezzar's Throne Room.

melted down and recast. This would be done not because their metal
was flawed or their tone untrue, but because God had a different carol
for them to peal. In those final, awful days of Jerusalem's death throes,
Jeremiah had looked beyond the corporate guilt of his people and the
corporate suffering which would shortly fall upon them, and had spoken
of God's ways with individual men and women (Jer. 31:27f.). It was an
aspect of Israel's faith which had been implicit from the very beginning
of her dialogue with God, but Jeremiah had signaled that the day would
come when it would fill a new need in the life of the nation.

Ezekiel's spiritual instincts now told him that that day was at hand.
In a remarkable declaration in which he tells of experiencing a near

rebuke by God for his former oracles over Jerusalem's communal guilt and punishment, he intones a proclamation of spiritual independence.

> The word of the LORD came to me again: "What do you mean by repeating this proverb concerning the land of Israel, 'The fathers have eaten sour grapes and the children's teeth are set on edge'? As I live, says the Lord GOD, this proverb shall no more be used by you in Israel. Behold, all souls are mine; the soul of the father as well as the soul of the son is mine; the soul that sins shall die. . . . When the son has done what is lawful and right, and has been careful to observe all my statutes, he shall surely live. . . . The son shall not suffer for the iniquity of the father, nor the father suffer for the iniquity of the son; the righteousness of the righteous shall be upon himself, and the wickedness of the wicked shall be upon himself."
>
> (Ezek. 18:1–4, 19b, 20b; cf. Jer. 31:29f.)

It was a new freedom before God which Ezekiel urged. The nation had sinned and the nation had been purged. But now men and women of faith could slough off the nation's guilt and could respond to God's love in deeply intimate and personal ways. And God would acknowledge this in equally personal fashion.

In this fresh climate Ezekiel continued to dream, but his visions were now permeated with this new orientation of hope. The days of death were over. Israel had achieved a nadir from which God would lift her to new life. And it must not be forgotten that the doing was God's and not Israel's.

> The hand of the LORD was upon me, and he brought me out by the Spirit of the LORD, and set me down in the midst of the valley; it was full of bones. . . . Then he said to me, "Son of man, these bones are the whole house of Israel. Behold, they say, 'Our bones are dried up, and our hope is lost; we are clean cut off.' Therefore prophesy, and say to them, Thus says the Lord GOD: Behold, I will open your graves, and raise you from your graves, O my people; and I will bring you home into the land of Israel. And you shall know that I am the LORD, when I open your graves, and raise you from your graves, O my people. And I will put my spirit within you, and you shall live, and I will place you in your own land; then you shall know that I, the LORD, have spoken, and I have done it, says the LORD."
>
> (Ezek. 37:1, 11–14)

Yet God had far greater designs upon Israel than simply the resuscitation of a corpse. It was to be to a new order of life that God would resurrect his people, a life of harmony and love in which God ruled the people through the agency of the Davidic king and in which God's compassionate commandments would be inscribed upon the soul of the people. In Ezekiel's oracles describing this new life one plainly hears the echoes of the words of Jeremiah and of the cadences of Psalm 23. But these are combined with Ezekiel's own inspired phrases in such a way that his colleagues of the exile, who remembered his previous words of gloom, looked up from their water wheels and their scythes, and took hope.

> For thus says the Lord GOD: Behold, I, I myself will search for my sheep, and will seek them out. As a shepherd seeks out his flock when some of his sheep have been scattered abroad, so I will seek out my sheep; and I will rescue them from all the places where they have been scattered on a day of clouds and thick darkness. And I will bring them out from the peoples, and gather them from the countries, and will bring them into their own land; and I will feed them on the mountains of Israel, by the fountains, and in all the inhabited places of the country. I will feed them with good pasture, and upon the mountain heights of Israel shall be their pasture; there they shall lie down in good grazing land, and on fat pasture they shall feed on the mountains of Israel. I myself will be the shepherd of my sheep, and I will make them lie down, says the Lord GOD. I will seek the lost, and I will bring back the strayed, and I will bind up the crippled, and I will strengthen the weak, and the fat and the strong I will watch over; I will feed them in justice.
>
> (Ezek. 34:11–16)

> A new heart I will give you, and a new spirit I will put within you; and I will take out of your flesh the heart of stone and give you a heart of flesh. And I will put my spirit within you, and cause you to walk in my statutes and be careful to observe my ordinances. You shall dwell in the land which I gave to your fathers; and you shall be my people, and I will be your God.
>
> (Ezek. 36:26–28)

> And I will set up over them one shepherd, my servant David, and he shall feed them: he shall feed them and be their shepherd. And I, the LORD, will be their God, and my servant David shall be prince among them; I, the LORD, have spoken.
>
> (Ezek. 34:23f.)

Figure 24. Procession of Captives. Assyrian Frieze.

The Death of Ezekiel

In 572 the fortress of Tyre, which had endured the seige lines and the battering rams of Nebuchadrezzar for thirteen years, caved in before the patient Babylonian determination. Death by sword was perhaps a gratifying release to many who were wasted by starvation and disease, while others were compelled into the less lethal, but more painful, trek to Babylon, where they joined the captive Jews and the exiled remnants of other subject peoples in bondage. Some of Ezekiel's compatriots remembered his words about Tyre and were reminded afresh of the prophet's vision of the holiness and the universal rule of the God whom they worshipped (Ezek. 27).

Not long afterward Ezekiel dreamed his ultimate and most splendid dream about God and His people (Ezek. 40–48). It was a vision of the Jerusalem Temple, so lovingly recalled from the days of his youth, in which details of the structure itself proved so vivid as almost to render the vision into an architectural catalogue. God himself was present in conversation with the prophet, and Ezekiel looked on as God measured the building and reasserted its value as the point of contact between himself and his people. The Temple of Ezekiel's vision was, however, more than a building. It was an event of faith, grander and more dynamic than any material structure could ever prove to be. From the Temple flowed the River of Life, the vivifying presence of Israel's God who, as he had taken Judah's life, would restore it again.

> And he said to me, . . . wherever the river goes every living creature which swarms will live, and there will be very many fish; for this water goes there, that the waters of the sea may become fresh; so everything will live where the river goes.
>
> (Ezek. 47:8f.)

It was perhaps the last utterance of Ezekiel, the final vision of hope and restoration which he held before his people. The years of his life coincided with the most traumatic half-century Jerusalem had endured since it had been claimed by David's warriors as their own. That the trauma did not prove fatal must in no small measure be credited to Ezekiel. And as his cold body was laid in the warm Mesopotamian clay, his closest friends were already at work, transposing his words into written form, that future generations should know them and remember.

The Death of Nebuchadrezzar

Nebuchadrezzar's death a decade later was lamented with great and sustained ritual sadness, not merely because the monarch had presided over the machinery of state and its vast capacities for official grief-making, but also because many Babylonians had never known another ruler, and the loss of father figure and potentate at once fell with uncommon severity. If Nebuchadrezzar's countrymen could have foreseen the future, they would have wept the more, for with the king's death, Babylon's heart, although not yet her body, expired also.

The father of the New Babylonian Empire was succeeded by his son Amel-Marduk, or as the Old Testament knows him, Evil-merodach. The Jews of Babylon wondered what the new king's accession implied for their lives. And in Jerusalem, the royal scribes dutifully chronicled one of the new monarch's first acts of state in the hope that it might be the harbinger of better days for all of the people of God.

> And in the thirty-seventh year of the exile of Jehoiachin king of Judah, in the twelfth month, on the twenty-seventh day of the month, Evil-merodach king of Babylon, in the year that he began to reign, graciously freed Jehoiachin king of Judah from prison; and he spoke kindly to him, and gave him a seat above the seats of the kings who were with him in Babylon. So Jehoiachin put off his prison garments. And every day of his life he dined regularly at the king's table; and for his allowance, a regular allowance was given him by the king, every day a portion, as long as he lived.
>
> (2 Kings 25:27–30)

And on that quiet note the book of the Great History was closed.

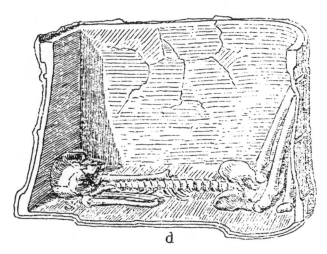

Figure 25. Babylonian Sarchophagus.

Chapter Five

Comfort, comfort my people,
says your God.
Speak tenderly to Jerusalem,
and cry to her
that her warfare is ended,
that her iniquity is pardoned,
that she has received from the LORD's *hand*
double for all her sins.

—Isaiah 40:1f.

Amel-Marduk[16]

In the sixth century B.C., well before the birth of human psychology
as a formal scientific discipline, it had not yet occurred to anyone to draw
a portrait of what happens to the minds and hearts of those sons who
grow to maturity in the shadows of extremely vigorous and aggressive
fathers. If it had, the analyst might well have alighted upon the person
of Amel-Marduk as the subject of such a case study. No contemporary
accounts of the new king's nature and activity have come down to us, but
it is possible to imagine through the mists a profile of Nebuchadrezzar's
son.

Born about the time of his father's accession to the throne not long
after Carchemish, the infant prince received a name befitting his future
as Babylon's king and—as it invoked Babylon's great god—a name reflecting the "official" piety of Nebuchadrezzar: the "Son of Marduk" he
was called, and he was thus designated a some-day defender of Babylon's
faith and sovereign of her destiny. His education was designed as carefully as his name, and to the same end. He was schooled by the priests to
participate in the liturgy, especially in the elaborate New Year's celebration in the autumn when, to the chanted strains of the ancient hymn of
creation, *Enuma elish,* Marduk was ceremonially enthroned in Esagila,
his temple. It was the very highest state occasion of the year, and the
participation of the king—Nebuchadrezzar was never absent—was the essential sign of the monarch's reconfirmation to rule for another twelve
months as the regent of the god.

Young Amel-Marduk was taught to master a horse by the finest of
Nebuchadrezzar's cavalry, was instructed in swordplay by officers of the

palace guard, and was trained in the essentials of military strategy by members of the general staff, including Nergal-shar-usur, the Rabmag. This soldier, the son of a private citizen of Babylon, possessed a martial skill which was generously braced by a lusty ambition, and he had gained membership into the royal household by winning the hand in marriage of Amel-Marduk's older sister, the princess royal.

The artisans and craftsmen who transformed Nebuchadrezzar's vast building schemes into reality were summoned to tutor the prince in the refinements of their arts; the royal scribes taught him to read the awkward cuneiform script and allowed his hands to impress into soft, yielding clay the wedge-shaped styli; and the astrologer-priests unfolded before him the mysteries of the heavens. When the boy grew older, he accompanied his father on his frequent excursions through the realm. As the imperial standards were displayed and tribute monies gathered, the crown prince took the measure of his future subjects and they of him. Occasionally, when the decision was not in doubt, Amel-Marduk accompanied his fierce sire into battle, pursuing bandits who preyed on border communities, or subduing subjects rendered recalcitrant by poverty. He also examined the seige lines around Jerusalem and around Tyre and, in colorful reviews, took the salute of Babylon's crack battalions. In the manifold means by which royal fathers have trained their successor-sons through the long stretches of civilized history, Nebuchadrezzar groomed Amel-Marduk to be the lord of Babylon.

All the while the crown prince held himself in readiness and trained his royal faculties. And the longer he trained, the older he grew, until it seemed that training and waiting and growing older had formed a rhythmic undulation which would transport him through life. His father was never ill, rarely fatigued, always alertly immersed in the affairs of empire and, as year succeeded year, it grew increasingly difficult to imagine that it could ever be any other way. Adolescence came and went for Amel-Marduk, as did early adulthood. And moving beyond maturity into the first reaches of middle life, the crown prince became distracted. His skills of statecraft were overhoned. He drilled for a contingency which never came. And growing to despise his continuing rehearsal for splendor, he found compensation in other haunts of the soul. Perhaps it was music which wooed him, or prayer. Whatever it was, when Nebuchadrezzar suddenly died in early October of 562, Amel-Marduk, nearing the fifth decade of his life, inherited a throne which he did not want and which he would not master.

The weakness of the new king was not immediately apparent, except perhaps to the members of his own family and to the more important of the royal advisors. So efficient was the machinery of state which Neb-uchadrezzar had forged, that it easily and effectively ran on its own momentum for the several weeks of official mourning over the death of the old king and of official rejoicing over the coronation of the new. It was, in fact, more than a year before rumor took note of the unhappy fact that no propulsion to the vehicle of state issued from above; and the more his subjects now discussed the king's dalliance, the more obvious that dalliance became. The first protests, of course, were from the military. The Babylonian army, charged with the delicate task of imposing order upon a vast and yeasty population, was sensitive to all signs of infirmity in the imperial structure. Any lack of resolve on the part of the monarch was sure to coax rebellion from one quarter or another, and the generals fidgeted and fumed over the relaxed aimlessness of the king.

As the second anniversary of Amel-Marduk's coronation approached, clashes and alarums on the imperial borders grew more frequent, as did seditious conspiracies among the subject peoples within the kingdom. And the general staff, in whispered, covert conversations, decided that the necessary blow must be struck. Nergal-shar-usur was, in all eyes, the logical candidate to usurp the royal power. His loyalty to Babylon had been proved by more than three decades of military activity which had included service in the second Jerusalem campaign (Jer. 39:13) as well as in combat before Tyre. Always a favorite of Nebuchadrezzar, this clever commoner had smoothly risen to the top of the scale of command and, as the husband of the princess royal, had attracted a certain regal aura to himself. Now his genuine concern over the erosive effect upon Babylonian power of Amel-Marduk's executive feebleness was fanned by his own voracious ambition.

On a warm August evening in 560, a handful of general officers, armed with a consenting nod from Nergal-shar-usur, made their way into the king's bedchamber and stole his life. There was some scuffling between regular army and sentinels of the palace guard, but peace was quickly restored and Babylon awoke at dawn to welcome a new king.

The Jewish community in Babylon surveyed these events with a more than dispassionate fascination. It had now been a quarter century since the final, dreadful collapse of Jerusalem, and many changes had found a way into their lives. As the proportion of Babylon-born Jews increased by virtue of the natural rhythms of birth and death, an acceptance of life beside the Euphrates grew more widespread. To many the land seemed less forlorn, their masters less hostile. The security with which Babylonian military muscle cushioned this heart of Nebuchadrezzar's empire gave to their lives a large measure of regularity and order. The

Figure 26. Artist's Reconstruction of a Babylonian Street Scene.

dark loam, moistened by Nebuchadrezzar's canals, gave up lush, nutritious grain, and in the villages, in Babylon itself, Jewish goods were easily exchanged for coin of the realm.

The early fears of ethnic disintegration were abandoned now. No longer did the captives feel so sharply the pressures to renounce their own identity by adopting Babylonian ways. They could live like the Jews they were, remembering their own history, shaping—within limits—their own experiences, and planning their own future. And it was now clear that there would be a Jewish future, although its dimensions were the subject of uncertainty, even argumentation. There were not a few Jews who could think of no other hope than the restoration of the people to their own land. These men and women, who were by no means only the more senior exiles, spoke openly and lovingly of Jerusalem, lamented her present brokenness, and equated God's salvation with her rebuilding and their return to her. Others, the majority, spoke with equal confidence of the future, but envisioned it in Babylonian, not Judean, terms. For these Jews, the future had, in a sense, already arrived, for they were part of a prosperous order which thrived on the domestic tranquility of the moment, and their status as captives was virtually forgotten in the rewarding undulation of their everyday lives. The words of Jeremiah, of Ezekiel, and of the Great History—which was perused as closely in Babylon as in Jerusalem—had made their mark. Israel's yesterdays were comprehensible as expressions of the justice of God and her tomorrows would be orchestrated by his mercy and love. If the score was yet a matter for debate, the very discussion over it was a symptom of the vigorous hope on which Babylonian Jewry now thrived.

The more they hoped, the more the Jews of the exile drank from the streams which fed that hope. The words of the seers of old, not just favorites like Jeremiah and Ezekiel, but others of more ancient memory like Isaiah and Micah of Jerusalem, like Amos and Hosea of Samaria— these words were read and reread, each exposure to them forging fresh links between the Jews of the exile and the prophets' God with his ways of radical judgment and grace. As the words were read, they were also reproduced by those who fell under their awesome spell, copied in order that each enclave of exiles, each cluster of worshipping Jews meeting for prayer in homes or in larger, especially appointed places, might also read and digest the promises and threats of old. The copying was not always slavishly done, letter for letter. Rather the old oracles were often shaped and nuanced, the more directly to bear upon the needs of the moment, as the exiles viewed those needs. And they were expanded by scribal insertions, the words of a particular prophet inspiring proclamations on the part of those who thought of themselves as his disciples and interpreters. As the record of God's ancient conversation with his people was enlarged in this way to be applied to new urgencies, the expansions were judged by the exiled community to be no mere addendum to the past, but as part of the continuing dialogue of God with his people.

While the Jews of Babylon watched, the body of the luckless Amel-Marduk was laid away with sumptuously hypocritical pomp. Those who saw the Jewish future here, athwart the Euphrates, trembled that their stable social order might now face new assaults. Meanwhile those who longed for Jerusalem hoped for some convulsion to expell them toward home.

The Holiness Code[17]

In the earliest days of exile no group, the Judean royal family aside, had suffered more than the Temple priests. Like Ezekiel, who was one of their number, large groups of priests had been marched to Babylon in both deportations and here, in this forbidding environment, deprived of cult and Temple, their theology of the uniqueness of the city and the sanctuary of God under severe strains, they struggled to come to terms with their faith and with their vocation as celebrants of the sacred presence of God. They did so by substituting for the Temple and for the liturgy practiced there an energetic reaffirmation of the legislation upon which both Temple and liturgy were based. It was a bold and creative strategy, one which finds few parallels in human history. Denied the most appropriate and satisfying means of expressing their faith—prayer and sacrifice in the Jerusalem Temple—they asserted all the more vigorously the ideological and philosophical underpinnings of that faith, Israel's

Figure 27. The Assyrian King's Foresters.

body of cultic and liturgical law. If it appeared to sceptics as an effort to shore up the foundations after the house had been knocked down, the priests seem not to have minded. Israel's ancient codes of liturgy and cult, carried by scrap and fragment over the sands to Babylon, were dusted off and addressed with heightened enthusiasm. Read and declaimed in periods of worship, the laws seized large, fresh chunks of the Jewish soul and, in order to facilitate its study and use, the priests began to arrange and systematize the mass according to subject and function.

One such legal catalogue forged by the priests of the exile is to be seen embedded in the text of the Book of Leviticus (Lev. 17–26). The theme is the holiness of God, and around this compelling motif are arranged a variety of ancient statutes and proscriptions—many as old as Israel itself—which apply to a wide spectrum of life: sexual relations, witchcraft, theft, hospitality to strangers, blasphemy, the breeding of cattle. But most of the emphasis is upon the liturgy of worship and upon those who presided over that liturgy: the members of the priesthood must be hygenically pure; the festivals of the cultic year—Passover, Sabbath, First Fruits, Atonement, and Booths—must be punctually and appropriately kept; and the sacramental bread must be baked to the measurements of a precise recipe. The reason for all of this is clear. Like a Greek chorus, the catalogue of laws intones over and again that "I, the Lord, am holy." And because that is so, God's people must be holy as well.

> Consecrate yourselves therefore, and be holy; for I am the LORD your God. Keep my statutes, and do them; I am the LORD who sanctify you.
> (Lev. 20:7f.)

The priests of the exile, as they put the finishing touches to this Code of Holiness, etched into the corner of the canvas their own autograph. It was in the form of a rationale, an extended explanation in terms of their own liturgical theology of the disastrous collapse of Jerusalem and of their present exile. The reason for this calamitous turn to Israel's history was simply that the nation had neglected God's ordinances of cult and Temple and had, therefore, been banished from the land. The present discomfort was, in a sense, an effort by God to perpetuate a code of worship which his people had refused to keep. If they had disregarded the Sabbath, working their oxen and plows even on that sacred day,

> then the land shall enjoy its sabbaths as long as it lies desolate, while you are in your enemies land; then the land shall rest, and enjoy its sabbaths. As long as it lies desolate it shall have rest, the rest which it had not in your sabbaths when you dwelt upon it.
> (Lev. 26:34f.)

But even so, God had not forgotten his people nor cut them off from his love.

> Yet for all that, when they are in the land of their enemies, I will not spurn them, neither will I abhor them so as to destroy them utterly and break my covenant with them; for I am the LORD their God; but I will for their sake remember the covenant with their forefathers, whom I brought forth out of the land of Egypt in the sight of the nations, that I might be their God: I am the LORD.
>
> (Lev. 26:44f.)

In congregations of worshipping exiles, words like these were chanted and hymned, their thick sounds enriching the air like vicarious fumes of altar fires. Many who listened or sang pined for the return to flame and sacrifice, but others preferred the song.

Nergal-shar-usur[18]

Nergal-shar-usur quickly brought his considerable skills and energies to bear upon the problems at hand. With perhaps the prayerful meaning of his own name in mind—"Nergal [a Mesopotamian god] protect the king"—the new monarch immediately validated his right to rule by means of an appeal to the Babylonian pantheon. Insisting that the gods had appointed him "to wield authority over the black headed [i.e., Babylonian] people," he paraded himself as Nebuchadrezzar's rightful heir and spoke of the "true crown" conferred upon him by Marduk. Soon troops were moved against the regions of unrest inside the empire as well as those on its borders and, when a simple show of force was insufficient to cow the troublemakers into submission, Babylonian swords drew blood. The alliance with the Medes which both empires had found so useful during the long life of Nebuchadrezzar was renewed by Nergal-shar-usur, his wife's Median blood possibly being of some benefit to the new lord of Babylon in bringing the negotiations to a favorable conclusion.

The new ruler, who was already rich in currency and in land at the time of his accession, enlarged his properties in Babylon and elsewhere, an ancient palace within the city being claimed and renovated for the king's personal use. But Nergal-shar-usur had studied his father-in-law well and, after the fashion of Nebuchadrezzar, he ordained extensive projects of building and restoration for the public sector. The king refurbished the Esagila and Ezida temples in Babylon and Borsippa, respectively, renovated a sanctuary named "The Chapel of Destiny" on the eastern bank of the Euphrates, and dug or redug a number of canals and irrigation ditches around Babylon.

The aggressive vitality of Nergal-shar-usur is displayed most conspicuously, however, in a surviving fragment of the Babylonian Chronicle, the single piece of that history which briefly resumes the story of the New Babylonian Empire broken off by the loss of the tablets for the years after 594. According to this fragment, Nergal-shar-usur reacted strongly to certain hostile troop movements by Appuasu, the ruler of the small kingdom of Pirindu, located near the imperial frontier in what is today southeastern Turkey. The Babylonian army, under the personal command of the king, fell upon Appuasu and his forces and, in spite of an ambush set for them in a narrow mountain defile, routed the hostile battalions and gave chase to their fleeing king. Traveling over such precipitous terrain that it was necessary to march in single file for almost one hundred miles, the Babylonians under Nergal-shar-usur followed their enemy to his capital of Ura, which they invested. The city capitulated and was destroyed by the Babylonians, but Appuasu escaped to his ancestral home in Kirsu, deep in the mountains some forty miles to the west. Not to be denied, Nergal-shar-usur and the Babylonians resumed the chase, braving a hazardous mountain pass before assaulting the city and reducing it to ashes. But the wily Appuasu again evaded Nergal-shar-usur's grasp and disappeared for good into the mountain fastness.

Turning southward in frustrated fury, the Babylonians marched to the Mediterranean coast and, in an (for them) unusual amphibious operation, landed on an island fortress where Appuasu had stationed 6,000 fighting men. The fortress fell and its surviving defenders were marched off into captivity. The tablet concludes:

> In that year, from the pass leading to the city of Sallune as far as the boundary of the city of Ludu he [Nergal-shar-usur] burned with fire. Appuasu fled and his hand did not capture him. In the month of Adar the king of Akkad [i.e., Babylon] returned to his own land.[19]

The date was now 556, and Babylonian hearts pounded with pride that Nergal-shar-usur had, after the sad interlude under Amel-Marduk, restored the fortunes of empire with all of the elan of a resurrected Nebuchadrezzar. But fortune's wheel was well greased and had yet other turns to make. In the fourth year of his reign, at the height of his power, Nergal-shar-usur faltered and, with no formality at all, Babylon's lusty and ambitious king fell dead.

The Priestly History[20]

The priests who served the Jewish community in Babylon soon moved beyond the practice of cataloguing and commenting upon Israel's ancient laws. Catching sight of a grander vision of the accumulated sweep of God's ways with his people, they laid out upon the floor of Israel's spirit a vast mosaic of human history, a narrative which reached backward to the very first creative urgings of God and which traced the subsequent divine probings into the soul of man.

This splendid work of art was not all of a piece. Many of the colorful agates and granites had been cemented together long before, some in very distant days, into limited but self-contained portraits—miniature mosaics in their own right. Some of the priests' own anthologies, such as the Code of Holiness, were pressed *en bloc* into the cool mortar which bound the mosaic together; while many of the precisely cut individual stones were the work of the exiled priests or of their few remaining colleagues in Jerusalem. Most importantly, however, the larger pattern into which these bits, great and small, were gently forced emerged unmistakably from the minds and hearts of the Jewish priests in Babylon. It was a design which bore the stamp of their singular conviction: God had chosen Israel to be his own people, and by means of the precise rituals which he had ordained—rituals of which the priests themselves were the custodians and of which the worship in the Jerusalem Temple had formed the sharpest focus—God had provided the instruments by which Israel could express her acceptance of his love. The vast mosaic which the priests now began to lay was to be a diagram of this conviction, and all of the settings which went into it were to help give it its ultimate meaning and shape.

The priests were not, of course, ignorant of the lessons of the Great History, and in many respects their own splendid narrative supported its essential instruction. But the Priestly History cast, in other ways, longer lines, fishing right up to the waters of God's own primordial impulses. It also identified the very mechanics of Israel's liturgy and cult with the mind of God and proclaimed Israel's joy as her faithfulness to the divine legislation which enshrined liturgy and cult. If the Great History, with its concern for Israel's inner response to God's loving overtures, represented a "Protestant" view of Israel's story, the Priestly History, with its commitment to liturgical detail, stood as a "Catholic."

Nothing in the Priestly History was done haphazardly or without an eye upon its overall effect, the majestic drama of God's creation of the world serving as the most striking example of that fact. The priests of the exile were all too familiar with the Babylonian creation epic in which Marduk fashions the world out of the halved carcass of the evil dragon Tiamat, whom he has slain in fierce combat. And their collective experience also included contact with the Canaanite fertility myths, including that of the classic conflict between the deities Baal and Prince Sea.[21] But the priests' dramatic recital of the creation of the world by the God of Israel, while revealing their knowledge of Babylonian and Canaanite mythology, was on all counts their own. (The Hebrew for "deep," which is the nearest thing to an evil force in Genesis 1, is, by etymology, akin to the word "Tiamat"; and the presence of the primeval sea in the priestly epic is unmistakable.) There is no struggle by God, no effort at all, in fact. He simply speaks and creation majestically and silently explodes into being, the heavens bedazzled with lights, the earth vibrant with life.

Even the geometry of the epic reveals the symmetrical and polished execution by the priests of their liturgical ideals.

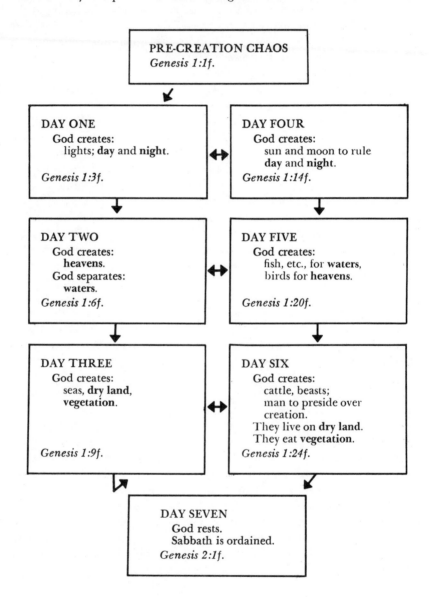

And so, according to the Priestly epic, even creation possesses a liturgical purpose. No sooner is man created than God provides him with one of the means by which he is to express his dependence upon and praise of God: the Sabbath.

> Thus the heavens and the earth were finished, and all the host of them. And on the seventh day God finished his work which he had done, and rested on the seventh day from all his work which he had done. So God blessed the seventh day and hallowed it, because on it God rested from all his work which he had done in creation.
>
> (Gen. 2:1-3)

From the smooth and magisterial narrative of creation, the Priestly History moves into the tales of the patriarchs, of Abraham, Isaac, Jacob and Joseph, and of the covenant which bound them and the nation which would spring from them to their God. It is this covenant which fascinated the priests and in which they saw the clue to the purpose of Israel's life. The occasion of its declaration by God to Abraham is related with careful detail and, as in the case of the epic of creation, the priests proposed a reminder of its importance in terms of their own ritual (Gen. 17). As the sabbath was to be kept in honor of God's deeds of creation, so each generation of Hebrew males would undergo circumcision as a mark of the abiding validity of God's covenant with Israel and as a physical reminder that God had embraced Israel as his own people, claiming for them the land in which Abraham and his sons had been only visitors: Canaan.

The Priestly History's next grand concern is the Exodus from Egypt. In this great act of liberation, God, who was solely responsible that it had happened at all, vindicated his promises made to Abraham and established those channels through which Israel might make vivid her devotion and commitment to him. The Passover is especially recalled as the festival of emancipation, the tribal loyalties are defined during the years in the wilderness, the elaborate rituals for the worship in the Tabernacle are laid out, the role of the priesthood is precisely described, and a vast body of legal material touching upon almost every aspect of human life and activity is recorded. Some of this material—the Ten Commandments, for example (Exod. 12:1-20)—seems basic to all times and types of human society, while other parts fall with a dull and pedantic thud upon the modern ear: the formulae concerning clean and unclean animals, the ceremonial purification of women after childbirth or following menstration, and the ritual bathing which must be performed after sexual intercourse; the codes governing burnt offering, sin offering, guilt offering, and peace offering; the tests for leprosy. But in the regard of the Priestly History even the ancient minutiae were part of the wall necessary to set

Israel apart from her pagan neighbors (as here in Babylon!) and, now that the Temple was gone, must constitute the house in which Israel met and worshipped her God. But imbedded in the midst of the building stones are ingots of gold:

> You shall not hate your brother in your heart, but you shall reason with your neighbor, lest you bear sin because of him. You shall not take vengeance or bear any grudge against the sons of your own people, but you shall love your neighbor as yourself: I am the LORD.
>
> (Lev. 19:17f.)

The final part of the Priestly History deals with the preparations for the entry into the Promised Land. The boundaries of the new nation are meticulously drawn, the territories of the several tribes are apportioned, and the cities of refuge are proclaimed where, under certain circumstances, fugitives from justice may find shelter from the harsher demands of the law (Num. 34f.; Josh. 13–19). Thereupon Moses, who has led his people through four decades of peril and danger, is carried by God to the peak of Mt. Nebo which overlooks the land and is permitted this single view of the haven toward which he has toiled so long (Deut. 32:48f.; 34:1, 7–9). And then the old man dies, a victim of his own sinfulness, while the leadership of the nation passes into other hands. It is they, not he, who will see the consummation of that which God promised as long ago as Abraham and planned as long ago as the creation of the world.

On that suspenseful note the Priestly History closes, and every Jew of the exile who read it would have recognized in it a homily for the times. As at the death of Moses, Israel now seemed poised on the brink of a portentous future. God's promises were still in effect, for Israel still lived. An older generation which had borne the brunt of death and destruction occasioned by the nation's sinful past was slipping away, their bodies cocooned in Mesopotamia's silent earth. And into the hands of their sons and daughters the responsibility for harvesting God's promises and implementing his demands was being thrust. And to them the priestly imperative was urgent and clear:

> If you walk in my statutes and observe my commandments and do them, then I will give you your rains in their season, and the land shall yield its increase, and the trees of the land shall yield their fruit. And your threshing shall last to the time of vintage; and the vintage shall last to the time for sowing; and you shall eat your bread to the full, and dwell in your land securely. And I will give peace in the land, and you shall lie down, and none shall make you afraid; and I will remove evil beasts from the land, and the sword shall not go through your land. And you shall chase your enemies, and they shall fall before you by the sword. . . . And I will have regard for you and make you fruitful and multiply you, and

will confirm my covenant with you. And you shall eat old store long kept, and you shall clear out the old to make way for the new. And I will make my abode among you, and my soul shall not abhor you. And I will walk among you, and will be your God, and you shall be my people. I am the LORD your God, who brought you forth out of the land of Egypt, that you should not be their slaves; and I have broken the bars of your yoke and made you walk erect.

(Lev. 26:3–13)

Nabonidus Rules Babylon[22]

The astrologer-priests of Babylon, who eagerly scanned the skies for divine portents, have left us no known record of their readings for the year 556. But we may be confident that their customary interrogation of the heavens was more intense than usual during that year and, had the planets and stars truly flashed messages, such communications would have left the astrologers bewildered and fearful. For the second time since the death of Nebuchadrezzar six years earlier, Babylon was awash in a crisis of power and rule.

The death of Nergal-shar-usur had deposited upon the throne his minor son Labashi-Marduk. The new king's royal credentials were proper enough, since he could claim the right to rule not only as the son of his father, but also—on his mother's side—as the grandson of Nebuchadrezzar. Yet the lad had the misfortune of inheriting Babylon's crown at a time when family conflict still smoldered from the brutal deposition of his uncle. And the question of who was to serve as regent over the empire during the young monarch's minority—and thus as the real power in the state—became a flashpoint of controversy and struggle among the descendants of Nebuchadrezzar. As it had during the period immediately after the death of the great king himself, Babylon dawdled, not as before through royal lassitude, but through royal bickering.

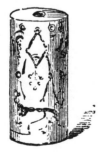 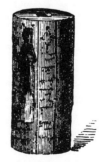

Figure 28. Babylonian Cylindrical Seals.

Other forces were also at work in Babylon in 556 of which, from our distance, we can detect only the most ghostly outlines. They were currents of emotion—political, economic, racial—which coursed through the life of the empire and threw up whirls and eddies of a most formidable nature. The vast Babylonian imperium now clutched to itself human beings of a wide variety of linguistic and racial stock, most of whom had, like the Jews, preserved their racial and cultural integrity and whose interests often clashed with those of one another and with those of Babylon herself. Not a few of these groups had contributed soldiers and administrators to the imperial machine, and thus the tensions and jealousies among them, and between them and Babylon, were often acted out in official circles. Time's ravages have obliterated from the surviving records the details of what was about to happen, but the dynamics of these various feuds—the squabbles within the royal family, the tensions festering among subject peoples—seem to be responsible for the fact that, with his reign less than one year old, Labashi-Marduk was overthrown and his scepter usurped by an outsider, an individual who was not only no descendant of Nebuchadrezzar, but who was not even Babylonian: a certain Nabonidus. A damaged inscription in basalt, found in Istanbul near the close of the last century, gives us our best, if hazy, clue to the forces which brought the new king to the throne:

> After his [Nergal-shar-usur's] days had become full and he had started on the journey of destiny [i.e., died], his son Labashi-Marduk, a minor who had not yet learned how to behave, sat down on the royal throne against the intention of the gods and . . . [the next three lines are destroyed].[23]

Nabonidus then goes on to describe how popular sentiment and the will of Babylon's great god Marduk had resulted in his coronation as the imperial monarch at the expense of the hapless boy king, who, presumably, was murdered.

Nabonidus was a native of Haran, where, it will be remembered, the last fragment of the Assyrian army had collapsed before a combined Babylonian and Median assault in 610. The city had thereafter found itself in that slice of the Assyrian pie which passed to the Medes, but, for reasons yet unclear, the family of Nabonidus had migrated to Babylon, perhaps brought there as a reward for their pro-Babylonian sympathies during the years of Nabopolassar's struggle to free his country from the Assyrian yoke. Nabonidus' mother, Adad-guppi, was a priestess of the moon god, Sin, whose worship was closely associated with Haran, and she was also, in all probability, of some kinship to the Assyrian royal family. Not only did this condition inject princely blood into the veins of her son, a quality upon which he doubtless presumed in legitimizing his *coup* against Labashi-Marduk, but it also implies a certain access to and familiarity with the courtly circles of Babylon by both mother and son.

Another legacy of Adad-guppi may well have been Nabonidus' qualities of physical stamina and—but for the course of events—his longevity. In her memoirs, composed in 550 at the age of 104 years, the priestess boasts of keen eyesight, excellent hearing, hands and feet in perfect condition, well articulated words, and a hearty appetite. She lived to see her 107th year of life and the ninth year of her son's rule.[24]

Whether Nabonidus' political and military judgment was as sound as the robust constitution he inherited from his mother, however, is another matter. The new monarch, who was nearly a septuaginarian upon his accession to the throne, seems, in spite of his age and apparent vitality, to have acted under the strong influence of his mother and that of other non-Babylonian elements who placed him there. One of his first acts of state was to march upon Haran with a large force, relieve the city of its Median overlords, and reestablish the sanctuary of Sin which the Medes had allowed to fall into decay. It was an act which, as Nabonidus' own inscriptions attest, was of special importance to him and (as it turned out) was to have fateful consequences for Babylon's future.

Three years into his rule the king performed an even more surprising maneuver. Entrusting the care of the government in Babylon to his eldest son, Bel-shar-usur (the biblical Belshazzar), Nabonidus led a sizeable military force south and west into the Arabian Desert and there pacified a series of oases on the important caravan routes into southern Arabia. In one of these, Tema, he constructed a second capital for himself of such strength and beauty that a later generation of scribes would compare it favorably to the royal palace in Babylon. For the better part of a decade Nabonidus was absent from the imperial city, either holding court in Tema or sweeping through other reaches of the realm at the head of a

Figure 29. Impression from a Persian Cylindrical Seal.

fearsome and colorful military retinue. The so-called Nabonidus Chron-icle, a cuneiform record of the monarch's seventeen-year reign written after his death and, it must be stressed, by his enemies, records with re-lentless repetition these continuing absences of the king from his duties in Babylon:

> Eleventh year: the king stayed in Tema; the crown prince, the officials, and his army were in Akkad. The king did not come to Babylon, Bel [i.e., Marduk] did not go out from Esagila in procession, the festival of the New Year was omitted, but the offerings for the gods of Babylon and Borsippa were given according to the complete ritual.[25]

It is quite impossible to explain this apparent distraction of the king. One view is that his preoccupation with the south was a kind of religious mission or retreat motivated by the same spiritual impulses which had led Nabonidus to rebuild the temple of Sin at Haran. In support, the discovery of evidence of the worship of Sin by natives of the Arabian Desert at a time slightly later than Nabonidus has been claimed. But such worship, if related to Nabonidus at all, could just as easily have been a by-product of his stay in Arabia as it could have been its principal motivation.

An explanation in commercial terms is perhaps on firmer ground. With a shifting and increasingly volatile military situation in the Median em-pire to the north and east, Nabonidus may have felt all the more strongly the need to maintain free and unimpaired trade routes to the Red Sea and the lands beyond. Only such a preoccupation, it may be argued, could justify his prolonged absence from Babylon.

Whatever his reasons, Nabonidus' neglect of official routine in Baby-lon grated against the sensitivities of powerful elements within the state who were presumably not well disposed towards him to begin with and whose irritation and hostility grew with the lengthening duration of his leave from the imperial city. Among those whom the king alienated would have been certain elements within the army and within the class of professional administrators and bureaucrats. In their eyes, Prince Bel-shar-usur's management of the city may have been well intentioned enough, but certain matters of military and political detail required the judgment of the king himself, and valuable time and advantage were often lost while imperial messengers covered the miles between Babylon and Tema to fetch the king's word.

But no group was more put off by Nabonidus' behavior than the priests of the royal city. Polytheism might be a way of life within the empire, and religious toleration of a wide variety of sects and cults the official posture of the state, but a special relation had always existed between the monarchy and those gods whose shrines were in Babylon—

especially the great god Marduk and
other deities with whom he was closely
associated. It takes little imagination
to conjecture the irritation kindled
among the Babylonian priests by Nabonidus' attentions to the cult of Sin
at Haran. And his continued absence
from the New Year celebration in
Babylon not only implied a personal
disregard for Marduk and the pantheon satellite to him, but it was also
a way of affirming in no very subtle
terms Nabonidus' presumption that he
possessed a right to rule which was
divorced from any blessing by those
deities—a grave heresy, political and
spiritual, in Babylonian eyes! In bal-
ancing the picture it must be said that
Nabonidus' many building inscriptions do not fail to mention his attentions to and concern for the shrines
and temples of the Babylonian gods.

Figure 30. Marduk.
From a Babylonian Engraving.

Such periodic efforts at maintenance and renovation, however, seem not
to have placated the rising annoyance of the priests of the imperial capital.

There is one footnote to Nabonidus' preoccupation with the oases of
Arabia, an item which falls into the category of a curiosity. Many years
later, almost all of the desert communities which Nabonidus mentions in
his inscriptions are found to contain small colonies of Jews. It is not
possible to assert, as one is tempted to do, that these are the descendants
of Jewish legionaires of the Babylonian army who came into the desert
with Nabonidus and stayed. Yet such a thing would not be entirely out
of reason, given what is likely to have been a high degree of Jewish in-
tegration into Babylonian life by the time of Nabonidus' reign.

The Rise of Cyrus[26]

In spite of the preoccupation of the Babylonian king with the south,
or perhaps partly because of it, developments which would prove of crucial importance to the future of Nabonidus and to his kingdom were
occuring in the north. The warlike Median empire, whose fierce as-
sistance to the Babylonians under Nabopolassar had proved so decisive
in the capture of the Assyrian capital, had witnessed a change in its for-

tunes. For one thing, the old alliance with the Babylonians, which had become no more than a formality, evaporated totally with the sack of Labashi-Marduk, the last Babylonian sovereign who could claim blood ties to the Median royal house. And Nabonidus' hasty annihilation of the Median garrison in Haran was the signal that a new day had arrived in the relationship between the two former friends.

A greater threat than the Babylonians suddenly surfaced, however, to trouble the Median ruler Astyages, one which took the sinister shape of his grandson, Cyrus, King of Persia. Cyrus was the son of Astyages' daughter Mandane, who had been given by the Median sovereign to Cambyses, the master of neighboring Persia, in the conventional and time-honored fashion by which princes cemented alliances between themselves. Little could Astyages have forseen that the fruit of this union would become the instrument of his own downfall. In one sense, Cyrus' aggression against his grandfather was the final, but not the most compelling, cause of the Median collapse. The older man had ruled from his capital of Ecbatana for more than a quarter of a century when Cyrus inherited the Persian throne upon the death of his father in 559. But, instead of mellowing with the years, a grace allowed many a monarch, Astyages grew dull and lazy. Luxury and idleness came to characterize the life of the Median court, and all of the old martial qualities which had fired the Median spirit a generation before now seemed as respected, but as remote, as the great mountains to the north. The meaning of the name of the pleasure loving old king, "Lance-hurler," appeared as inappropriate to his character as did the present flabby spirit of the nation to its muscular past.

Those arteries where the hot blood of the Medes of old still gushed were to be found in Cyrus. And not only was the young Persian the worthy heir of his Median forebears in terms of stamina and courage, but he was alert to the lack of these characteristics in others, particularly in his grandfather. Perhaps out of simple covetousness, but doubtless also out of the conviction that the Median kingdom would fall to the first invader (and why not keep the treasure in the family and out of the hands of potential enemies?), Cyrus marched westward from his own capital at Pasargadae and attacked his grandfather's royal residence at Ecbatana. To no one's surprise, except that of Astyages, large parts of the Median army went over to the side of Cyrus and delivered into the Persian hands their own chained and humiliated monarch.

The date of Cyrus' advance against Astyages and the duration of whatever conflict ensued are uncertain. The events may have occured as early as 556, the year of Nabonidus' accession. If that is so, the disturbance

could have proved of help to the Babylonian army under Nabonidus in
their assault upon a Haran whose Median defenders had been called
home to defend their king. On the other hand, the Nabonidus Chronicle
may be correct placing Cyrus' *coup*, or at least its successful conclusion,
in 549, a date by which Nabonidus had been in the south for three years.
In any event, a fresh and energetic force must now be reckoned with on
the military and political stage of the ancient near east. The Medes, rather
than being crushed by the Persians, were assimilated by them into a vast
new principality where both stood on an equal footing. Ecbatana became
a favorite summer residence of Cyrus and his court; Medes occupied central posts in government and in the military; and as late as the time of
the composition of the biblical Book of Daniel, more than three centuries
later, "the Medes and the Persians" were spoken of in a single breath
(Dan. 6:15; 8:20). Thus by at least 549, perhaps even earlier, Cyrus had
shrewdly amalgamated the energies of two of the ancient world's more
talented peoples and had taken the first steps toward erecting what was
to become a premier political structure in the history of Western civilization.

Now that Cyrus had drawn his first blood, his appetite was whetted
for further conquest. In logical fashion he moved with his Persian battalions, now beefed up by healthy contingents of Median fighters, into
the west in order to mop up the farther extremities of his grandfather's
former domain. The move sent chills of apprehension down the spines
of all of those who lived near his path and all of those, like the Babylonians, with interests vested there. Under the leadership of Croesus,
ruler of Lydia, whose kingdom lay athwart a fat slab of what is now modern Turkey, a hasty alliance was thrown together in which Egyptians,
Babylonians, and even the far-off Spartans on the Greek mainland,

Figure 31. Procession of Captives from a Assyrian Frieze.

pledged their help in frustrating the Persian march to the west. Such was the terror Cyrus had begun to generate in his world.

Croesus was himself not a man to be trifled with. He had inherited his father's throne only after a bloody contest with a half brother and had consolidated his position with military victories over such important Greek cities in Ionia as Ephesus and Miletus. However, it was in the development of trade and commerce that the Lydian king gathered an economic harvest which was even more imposing than that of his military power and which made him a figure of legendary proportions even while he lived. Cyrus, moving through the western reaches of Astyages' former kingdom and claiming the allegiance of its peoples, must have sniffed the aroma of Croesus' gold. By the time the Persian army climbed down from the cool Median highlands into the warm valley of upper Mesopotamia and sweetened its rations with the dates and olives which abounded there, Croesus had already plotted his moves, which, due to the exigencies of time, must be undertaken without his allies. And when Cyrus moved into Cappadocia, a land which had formerly served as a buffer between Lydians and Medians, he found Croesus waiting for him at the town of Pteria.

The battle which raged there was indecisive, as neither Lydian nor Persian armies swept the other from the field. But its aftermath tested the mettle of both antagonists and flashed to the world further evidence that in the Persian ruler there was a man who intended to bend events—and people—according to his will. After the battle Croesus retired to his capital, Sardis, near the Aegean coast, to regroup and refit his forces, obviously expecting that Cyrus would follow the conventional postulates of war and do the same. Instead of withdrawing to salve his wounds, however, Cyrus quickly followed Croesus into his own heartland and, taking the Lydians completely by surprise, swooped down on Sardis, stormed its defenses, and prostrated the city. According to one version of the events, as the Persian army fought in the streets of Sardis, Croesus unsuccessfully attempted to escape capture by immolating himself alive on a funeral pyre. But the Nabonidus Chronicle says simply that

> in the month Aiaru [Cyrus] marched against Lydia. . . . He killed its king, took his possessions, and put there a garrison of his own. Afterwards his garrison as well as the king remained.[27]

The time is now the spring of 547, and the Greeks and Persians have made their first fateful contact with one another. The conflict between these two resourceful peoples, which was to extend over the next 200 years, would provide history with some of its most brilliant and brutal moments of warfare, spark the first efforts at the authentic writing of

Figure 32. Impression from a Persian Cylindrical Seal.

history on the European continent, and sear into the universal human consciousness such names as Marathon, Thermopylae, and Salamis, together with the deeds of bravery and endurance which those names evoke.

The Babylonian Isaiah[28]

The full range of emotions which these events set loose in the hearts of the Jews in Babylon can only be conjectured, but it would seem consistent with all else that is known about the ferment of these days to surmise that the exiled community was no more of one mind about Cyrus and his energetic maneuvers than was the native citizenry of Babylon. Those Jews whose well-being was, in one fashion or another, pegged to the new administration of Nabonidus must have experienced the same disquiet as certain of their masters, for it took no clairvoyance to forsee that a clash of Persian and Babylonian arms was all but inevitable. If, as is by no means unlikely, Jewish elements now served in the Babylonian army, they especially would have had cause to grow nervous and depressed over the new menace from the north.

Other Babylonian Jews, however, found in Cyrus the reason for a strange kind of hope. The city of Babylon, languishing under the ill effects of Nabonidus' prolonged absence, was peppered through with a mood of dissent. Native priests who smarted under the imperial neglect of ritual and cult, military commanders and bureaucrats chafed by the awkward logistics imposed upon them by the distances to Tema, and merchants angered over the slimmed profit margins which times of political dislocation invariably induce, all grumbled and complained that only some new energy applied to the wheels of government from a fresh direction could bring redress. A few of the more brazen even courted treason by identifying that new energy with Cyrus, and in ill-concealed whispers they expressed a hope that the dynamic Persian might reinvigorate Babylon's life by claiming it for himself, in much the same way in which he had imparted fresh stimuli to the Medes. Those Babylonian Jews who saw their own future linked to the prosperity and peace of the city could be counted among these quiet insurgents and if, at this time, covert embassies from Babylon made contact with the Persian court, these Jews would have found no reason to object.

A third group of Babylonian Jews watched the fearsome progress of Cyrus and his omnivorous militia with unrestrained enthusiasm. These were those among the exiles whose view of Israel's place in history would never admit contentment until Jerusalem was restored and Israel's ancient ordinances and institutions reestablished there. These Jews represented no specific class among the exiles, but embraced every stratum: priests, merchants, scribes, farmers, soldiers, and all the rest. To them Cyrus embodied the best hope that their Babylonian captors would be crushed and that their freedom and the resurrection of their city would follow. Admittedly it was as yet a small hope, but the dizzying speed with which Cyrus had changed the balance of political and military power in that vast part of the world, and the strength of their faith in God's ancient promises, fanned into a warm and steady heat the coals of their hearts.

One of the Jews who held this hope most earnestly has left a record of the satisfaction with which he and certain other members of the exiled community looked upon Cyrus. This man was a scribe of the prophetic school, one of those who immersed themselves in Israel's rich lore of tradition and dictum from the past and who sought by means of their own reflection upon it to bring God's Word to bear upon his people's present circumstance. This man was knowledgeable of the broad spectrum of God's ancient conversation with Israel, but it was to the mighty Isaiah that he was drawn in a special exercise of obedience. As the disciple of that man of God who had lived and declared the divine Word in the Jerusalem of King Hezekiah two centuries before, this Jew of the exile addressed himself to the new initiatives which he saw that God was now beginning to make.

Like the Isaiah of old, he spoke of the magisterial presence of God in human affairs, of the Deity's abhorrence of human sin, and of how "the Holy One of Israel" would now, as he always had, forge human events into creations of his own design.

Have you not known? Have you not heard?
    Has it not been told you from the beginning?
    Have you not understood from the foundations of the earth?

It is he who sits above the circle of the earth,
    and its inhabitants are like grasshoppers;
who stretches out the heavens like a curtain,
    and spreads them like a tent to dwell in;
who brings princes to nought,
    and makes the rulers of the earth as nothing.

Scarcely are they planted, scarcely sown,
    scarcely has their stem taken root in the earth,
when he blows upon them, and they wither,
    and the tempest carries them off like stubble.

To whom then will you compare me,
    that I should be like him? says the Holy One.
Lift up your eyes on high and see:
    who created these?
He brings out their host by number,
    calling them all by name;
by the greatness of his might,
    and because he is strong in power
    not one is missing.

                                        (Isa. 40:21–26)

And as for the mighty Cyrus before whom kings and princes fall prostrate,
his doings are those of the Lord who has caused him to step forth at this
hour in order to achieve purposes of his own design.

Who stirred up one from the east
    whom victory meets at every step?
He gives up nations before him,
    so that he tramples kings under foot;
he makes them like dust with his sword,
    like driven stubble with his bow.
He pursues them and passes on safely,
    by paths his feet have not trod.
Who has performed and done this,
    calling the generations from the beginning?
I, the LORD, the first,
    and with the last, I am He.

                                        (Isa. 41:2–4)

Because his real name has not survived the centuries, later generations
were to come to know this anonymous prophet of God as the Babylonian
Isaiah, or the Second Isaiah, names which, although artificial, enshrine
his authentic prophetic stature and his spiritual kinship to the Isaiah of
old. His vision had been rendered keenly perceptive by the Spirit of God

and, as the events which he foresaw began to unfold, his declarations
were to kindle a sparkling expectancy among those of his fellow exiles
who listened.

The Fall of Babylon

When the clash between Cyrus and Nabonidus—long variously anticipated and feared—finally occurred, it was a climax so swift and decisive
as almost to make mockery of the months of tension and suspense which
preceded it. A catalogue of Cyrus' further excursions following those
events in the Greek city states of Ionia in 547 has not been preserved, but
one may presume that the kinetic Persian continued on the move. By
bluff, threat, and—when necessary—armed assault, the king added further
chunks of western Asia to the empire, and the same tactics were probably
equally successful at the eastern extremity of the kingdom. Thus by the
beginning of the year 539 Cyrus is likely to have controlled that enormous
bulk of terrain from the Aegean Sea to the Oxus River, more than 2,000
miles in extent and embracing a heretofore unimaginable wealth of people and treasure. At this point in his adventure Cyrus turned south, and
a huge assault force of Medes and Persians readied themselves for a descent upon Babylon.

At some time—no one knows precisely when—Nabonidus had become
alert to the danger which Cyrus presented to Babylon and to himself and
had left his desert habitat at Tema to return to the imperial city. There,
by the grace of the Nabonidus Chronicle, we catch a glimpse of him in
the seventeenth year of his reign performing—feverishly, it would seem—
all of those civic and liturgical duties which he had for long scorned. The
proper gods are worshipped according to the proper rubrics, the crucial
New Year's ritual is celebrated and, as if that weren't enough, gods from
other cities in the vicinity are brought to Babylon and adored. And all
the while the eyes of the king are fearfully fixed upon the large black
cloud smudging the northeastern sky.

In early October of 539 the storm broke. Opis, a Babylonian stronghold on the Tigris, some one hundred miles north of Babylon itself, became the object of a sharp Persian thrust. When the city fell under the
invading wave, the inhabitants of the regions to the south, through which
Cyrus would presumably march toward Babylon, revolted against the
imperial rule, a mischief for which many of them were unceremoniously
killed by the soldiers of Nabonidus. But time had expired for the last
king of the New Babylonian Empire. He and his few remaining loyal
troops fell back in disarray and on October 11, Sippar, halfway between
Opis and Babylon, fell without a fight. And two days later Persian troops
entered a Babylon ("their weapons packed away," in the words of the

Cyrus Cylinder) from which Nabonidus had fled. (The Cylinder was a skillful piece of propaganda composed under Persian sponsorship not long after Babylon's submission.)

Cyrus' treatment of the fallen city was gentle and respectful. Nabonidus was apprehended and, we may be sure, relieved of his life. But there was no looting and no destruction of Babylonian property, the sacred places were guarded by Persian soldiers against acts of sacrilege, and when Cyrus himself entered the city three days after its surrender ("green twigs were spread before him," trumpeted the Nabonidus Chronicle), he was quick to observe the religious and political niceties which Nabonidus had dismissed with such cavalier scorn. Marduk was elaborately worshipped by the Persian conqueror, political prisoners were set free, money was dispensed for long neglected public works, and the gods whom Nabonidus had in panic seized from neighboring communities were restored with appropriate prayers and hymns.

It was all a very clever and well orchestrated effort by Cyrus to win the sympathies of that sizeable part of the Babylonian population which had dissented from the heterodox rule of Nabonidus and which had seen in Cyrus the means of their deliverance. That it was a successful ploy there can be no doubt. The Cyrus Cylinder details the alleged injustices to Babylon's people and to her gods by Nabonidus, and continues:

> Marduk scanned and looked through all the countries, searching for a righteous ruler willing to lead him in the annual New Year's procession. Then he pronounced the name of Cyrus, king of Persia, and declared him ruler of all the world. He made the Guti country and all of the Manda-hordes bow in submission to Cyrus' feet. And Cyrus did always endeavor to treat according to justice the black headed peoples [i.e., the Babylonians] whom Marduk has made him conquer.[29]

Partly because Cyrus held the military trumps, but largely because they genuinely wanted to, the people of Babylon concurred and rejoiced.[30]

The Babylonian Isaiah and His Hope for Jerusalem's Restoration

The Babylonian Isaiah, who for almost a decade had bent his ear to all reports of the movements of Cyrus, could now abandon whatever inhibitions or needs for caution he had formerly felt and could identify by name the deliverer whom God had sent to release his people. The crucial nature of the moment and the virtually unparalleled role to which God had summoned Cyrus are shockingly spotlighted by the prophet, who reaches into the sacred vocabulary of God's dialogue with his people and applies to Cyrus a word which, in earlier times, had been used in a special way to describe God's sovereign authority over Israel through his regent, the Davidic king. The word was "messiah," later to have even more weighty implications for the people of God, but which for now means the "anointed" one, the especially designated human instrument who is to execute the will of God.

> Thus says the LORD to his anointed, to Cyrus,
>   whose right hand I have grasped
> to subdue nations before him
>   and ungird the loins of kings,
> to open doors before him
>   that gates may not be closed:
> "I will go before you
>   and level the mountains,
> I will break in pieces the doors of bronze
>   and cut asunder the bars of iron,
> I will give you the treasures of darkness
>   and the hoards in secret places,
> that you may know that it is I, the LORD,
>   the God of Israel, who call you by your name.
> For the sake of my servant Jacob,
>   and Israel my chosen,
> I call you by your name,
>   I surname you, though you do not know me.
>   (Isa. 45:1–4)

If his fellow exiles were astonished and offended by such strong, marginally blasphemous language, the Babylonian Isaiah could only reply that the matter was God's doing, not his own. And if such talk seemed too close to Cyrus' own boast that he was the tool of Marduk, why, that god's name should not even be breathed alongside the sacred syllables of the name of the Lord, God of Israel.

> I am the LORD, and there is no other,
>   besides me there is no God;
>   I gird you, though you do not know me,
> that men may know, from the rising of the sun
>   and from the west, that there is none besides me;
> I am the LORD, and there is no other.
> I form light and create darkness,
>   I make weal and create woe,
>   I am the LORD, who do all these things.
>   (Isa. 45:5–7)

He is a vague and evasive figure, this Babylonian Isaiah, and the modern student of his words cannot listen without feeling the urge to push back the shrouds which veil his face and personality and study the man himself—his family origins, his experiences of the spirit, his conversations with his fellow man, Babylonian as well as Jew—in order to identify those impulsions which drove him to his expansive and joyful visions and which helped give shape to his towering comprehension of God's schemes for Israel and for mankind. But to a greater degree than any other major prophetic figure, even more than the selfless Ezekiel, he is content to remain in the shadows in order that God's surprising new initiatives in the life of the people might be bathed in the full outburst of the light. We may be sure that his conviction that God was about to do some new thing had behind it a long history of meditation and prayer. His early disquiet over the vapidness and sheer stupidity of the idolatry practiced by his Babylonian masters resulted in perhaps the most stinging and sarcastic indictment of that form of worship ever penned.

> The ironsmith fashions it and works it over the coals; he shapes it with hammers, and forges it with his strong arm; he becomes hungry and his strength fails, he drinks no water and is faint. The carpenter stretches a line, he marks it out with a pencil; he fashions it with planes, and marks it with a compass; he shapes it into the figure of a man, with the beauty of a man, to dwell in a house. He cuts down cedars; or he chooses a holm tree or an oak and lets it grow strong among the trees of the forest; he plants a cedar and the rain nourishes it. Then it becomes fuel for a man; he takes a part of it and warms himself, he kindles a fire and bakes bread; also he makes a god and worships it, he makes it a graven image and falls down before it. Half of it he burns in the fire; over the half he eats flesh, he roasts meat and is satisfied; also he warms himself and says, "Aha, I am warm, I have seen the fire!" And the rest of it he makes into a god, his idol; and falls down to it and worships it; he prays to it and says, "Deliver me, for thou art my god!"
>
> (Isa. 44:12–17)

But the Babylonian Isaiah was not bent upon mocking, chastising, or blaming either the Babylonians or his own wayward people. He sensed that God was leading Israel to undertake dazzling new adventures. Im-

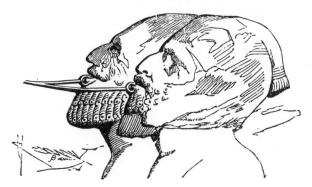

Figure 33. Assyrian Captives.

mersed in the lessons of his prophetic forebears, he attributed, as had
they, the torments and loneliness of exile and the humiliation of Jerusalem's collapse to Israel's breach of faith with God and to her sinful
abandonment of those moral and spiritual ideals to which He had summoned her. Yet that tragic drama was now over. New churnings of the
Spirit of God could be sensed, singular vibrations that the God of Israel
was again on the move. The sins of the past were over, purged, forgiven!
And a bright aurora pulsated just below the darksome horizon.

> Comfort, comfort my people,
>   says your God.
> Speak tenderly to Jerusalem,
>   and cry to her
> that her warfare is ended,
>   that her iniquity is pardoned,
> that she has received from the LORD's hand
>   double for all her sins.

> A voice cries:
> "In the wilderness prepare the way of the LORD,
>   make straight in the desert a highway for our God.
> Every valley shall be lifted up,
>   and every mountain and hill be made low;
> the uneven ground shall become level,
>   and the rough places a plain.
> And the glory of the LORD shall be revealed,
>   and all flesh shall see it together,
> for the mouth of the LORD has spoken."
>   (Isa. 40:1–5)

No local eruption this. No quiet, muted restoration of an ancient
people to their ancient land. The very Creator of the heavens and earth,
he who summons the stars to burn and the sea to roar, is doing a new
thing. And creation itself will lead the applause.

> Sing for joy, O heavens, and exult, O earth;
>   break forth, O mountains, into singing!
> For the LORD has comforted his people,
>   and will have compassion on his afflicted.
>   (Isa. 49:13)

Where in all of the years of God's union with his people is any com-
parable deed to be found? Nowhere, insisted the Babylonian Isaiah; there
is simply no duplicate of what God is about to accomplish. But if one
should insist upon a model, a paradigm, then the Exodus from Egypt
offers the nearest example. Then, as now, freedom had issued from bondage, joy had emerged from despair, and life was snatched from the
caverns of death.

Thus says the LORD,
    your Redeemer, the Holy One of Israel:
"For your sake I will send to Babylon
    and break down all the bars,
    and the shouting of the Chaldeans will be turned
        to lamentations.
I am the LORD, your Holy One,
    the creator of Israel, your King."
Thus says the LORD,
    who makes a way in the sea,
    a path in the mighty waters,
who brings forth chariot and horse,
    army and warrior;
they lie down, they cannot rise,
    they are extinguished, quenched like a wick:
"Remember not the former things,
    nor consider the things of old.
Behold, I am doing a new thing;
    now it springs forth, do you not perceive it?
I will make a way in the wilderness and rivers in
      the desert.
The wild beasts will honor me,
    the jackals and the ostriches;
for I give water in the wilderness,
    rivers in the desert,
to give drink to my chosen people,
    the people whom I formed for myself
    that they might declare my praise.

                    (Isa. 43:14–21)

The name of Cyrus is again invoked, and once more the Persian king's shoulders are adorned with the cloak of the Hebrew kings of old. Remembering the imagery often identified with the house of David, the Babylonian Isaiah vests in Cyrus the title "shepherd," the divinely chosen guardian of the flock of God. His pastoral purpose is to be quite specific: by virtue of his authority Jerusalem is to be rebuilt and the Temple of God restored.

Thus says the LORD, your redeemer,
    who formed you from the womb:
"I am the LORD, who made all things,
    who stretched out the heavens alone,
    who spread out the earth, . . .

who says of Jerusalem, 'She shall be inhabited,'
    and of the cities of Judah, 'They shall be built,
    and I will raise up their ruins';
who says to the deep, 'Be dry,
    I will dry up your rivers';

who says of Cyrus, 'He is my shepherd,
and he shall fulfil all my purpose';
saying of Jerusalem, 'She shall be built,'
and of the temple, 'Your foundation shall be laid.' "
(Isa. 44:24–28)

But let no one, especially the exiles themselves, misread the message. Israel's redemption is not to be an end in itself, however attractive such a prospect might seem to the Jews of Babylon. God harbors a larger purpose in his design upon the nations, that, by means of Israel's restored presence within the family of mankind, the knowledge of God's authority over history and the sensation of his love will be lodged in the larger heart of the human race.

Thus says God, the LORD,
who created the heavens and stretched them out,
who spread forth the earth and what comes from it,
who gives breath to the people upon it
and spirit to those who walk in it:
"I am the LORD, I have called you in righteousness,
I have taken you by the hand and kept you;
I have given you as a covenant to the people,
a light to the nations,
to open the eyes that are blind,
to bring out the prisoners from the dungeon,
from the prison those who sit in darkness.
I am the LORD, that is my name;
my glory I give to no other,
nor my praise to graven images.
Behold, the former things have come to pass,
and new things I now declare;
before they spring forth
I tell you of them."
(Isa. 42:5–9)

If the vapors of mystery cloud the identity of the Babylonian Isaiah and the details of his biography, they are joined by a second conundrum even more baffling. There exist, embedded in the text of his oracles, a series of poetic fragments—four by most reckonings—which have evoked intense scrutiny and thought (Isa. 42:1–4; 49:1–6; 50:4–9; 52:13–53:12). They are of a piece with the literature which surrounds them in that they share with it a common spiritual and ideological outlook and much common vocabulary. But they are distinct from that literature by describing the offices of a certain "Servant of the Lord," and by doing so in a literary style which often hints at a different human mind, or at least a different mood in the same mind, as that behind the other oracles of the Babylonian Isaiah. Further puzzlement is introduced by the fact that, while no two of these poems view the "servant" in the same light (he is now aggressive, then submissive; here he is triumphant, there is he destroyed), they are on common ground in identifying him as a means by which God's intentions, not just for Israel, but for all mankind, will be executed.

Who is this "Servant of the Lord"? What personality of the late sixth century B.C. did the Babylonian Isaiah or someone else of the same cast of spirit identify as this unique individual through whose virile, even war-like, but suffering presence God would touch the race of man? Cyrus? The Babylonian Isaiah himself? The nation Israel? Some contemporary whose name has now been lost? Some future figure who was yet to be born?

There have been nearly as many answers as there have been those who raised the question. But the piercing rhythms of the "Servant Poems" continue to this day to probe the mind of the reader and to plumb the depths of his soul.

> Surely he has borne our griefs
>   and carried our sorrows;
> yet we esteemed him stricken,
>   smitten by God, and afflicted.
> But he was wounded for our transgressions,
>   he was bruised for our iniquities;
> upon him was the chastisement that made us whole,
>   and with his stripes we are healed.
> All we like sheep have gone astray;
>   we have turned every one to his own way;
> and the Lord has laid on him
>   the iniquity of us all.
>
>   (Isa. 53:4–6)

Whomever the writer of these words may have intended to describe, they were ultimately to deliver a meaning which no one in the world of the sixth century B.C.—perhaps even the Babylonian Isaiah himself— could have fully foreseen.

IV.

RESTORATION

(538 B.C. and after)

Thus says Cyrus king of Persia: The LORD, *the God of heaven, has given me all the kingdoms of the earth, and he has charged me to build him a house at Jerusalem, which is in Judah. Whoever is among you of all his people, may his God be with him, and let him go up to Jerusalem, which is in Judah, and rebuild the house of the* LORD, *the God of Israel—he is the God who is in Jerusalem; and let each survivor, in whatever place he sojourns, be assisted by the men of his place with silver and gold, with goods and with beasts, besides freewill offerings for the house of God which is in Jerusalem.*

—Ezra 1:2–4

Chapter Six

The word of the LORD *came a second time to Haggai on the twenty-fourth day of the month, "Speak to Zerubbabel, governor of Judah, saying, I am about to shake the heavens and the earth, and to overthrow the throne of kingdoms; I am about to destroy the strength of the kingdoms of the nations, and overthrow the chariots and their riders; and the horses and their riders shall go down, every one by the sword of his fellow. On that day, says the* LORD *of hosts, I will take you, O Zerubbabel my servant, the son of Shealtiel, says the* LORD, *and make you like a signet ring; for I have chosen you, says the* LORD *of hosts."*

—Haggai 2:20–23

Cyrus' Decree[31]

The spindly Jewish farmer leaned against the flank of his ox, just freed from the traces which had bound it and its mate to the plow throughout this fine spring day, and with careful scrutiny eyed the column of men and horses which snaked along the road adjacent to his field. The procession was no more than thirty yards away and the deep western sun at the plowman's back inundated both the beasts and their riders in a wash of amber and caused the basest metal in their livery to burn with gold. The farmer involuntarily smoothed his wind-ruffled beard, patted the rump of his animal, and absorbed the details of this strange parade. It bore the mark of a certain military precision: an erect, sharp-nosed officer, astride a splendid sorrel stallion, rode at the head of the gently bobbing line; another dozen or so uniformed cavalrymen were to be seen at random intervals throughout the length of the column; and the proud standards of the Persian Empire—resplendent winged bulls adorned by human heads—floated above the men and horses, like pendants from the masts of some elongated, continuously flexing man o' war.

Yet this was no army, for women and children, crowded into large, creaking wagons, seemed as numerous as men, and the postures in the saddle of many of the riders and their obvious ineptitude at handling a horse betrayed their lack of familiarity with their present activity. Apart from the soldiers, there was no uniformity of dress, clothing of the coarsest kind hanging from the frames of most of the civilians. But an occasional flash of crimson silk bespoke more expensive attire, and one small cluster of males who joggled along immediately behind the Persian officer sported a variety of shimmering leather and smoothly embroidered satins which blended well with their superior horsemanship.

Within the span of twenty minutes the column had clattered by, leaving its dusty cloud suspended in the quiet, early evening air. As his shadow and that of the oxen grew longer and were finally swallowed by the gathering night, the Jewish farmer stood in his field absorbed in thought and testing the several sensations which crowded his brain. The identity of the procession, whose members would by now be making their camp just outside the ruined walls of Jerusalem, was no mystery to him, nor would it be to any citizen of the city who, at first light, would witness the column's noisy entrance into the city proper. The Persians, whose first patrols had bloodlessly swept through the region soon after the capitulation of Babylon, had been quite open about their intentions. Not more than six weeks before, a troop of Persian horse had jangled into the city with a copy of a royal proclamation which, the Persian captain had insured the community's leaders, would be welcome news indeed. But its terse Aramaic phrases, reeled off in the soldier's thick accent, had sired more than the predicted happy response.

> In the first year of Cyrus the king, . . . a decree: Concerning the house of God at Jerusalem, let the house be rebuilt, the place where sacrifices are offered and burnt offerings are brought; its height shall be sixty cubits and its breadth sixty cubits, with three courses of great stones and one course of timber; let the cost be paid from the royal treasury. And also let the gold and silver vessels of the house of God, which Nebuchadnezzar took out of the temple that is in Jerusalem and brought to Babylon, be restored and brought back to the temple which is in Jerusalem, each to its place; you shall put them in the house of God.
>
> (Ezra 6:3–5)

It was part of the new imperial policy, the officer had explained. Religious and cultural differences were not only to be tolerated by the mighty Cyrus, but even encouraged. The emperor had himself restored the gods which Nabonidus had looted from those Mesopotamian cities then at his mercy; and other more distant reaches of the old Babylonian imperium, whose grievances were of even longer standing, were to be afforded a similar courtesy. The Jews, of course, possessed no idols or images, but there was the matter of the pillaged Temple treasures lost to Nebuchadrezzar in 598, to say nothing of the Temple itself, a heap of ugly debris this half century now. These were to be restored by virtue of Cyrus' own munificent will.

But the largesse of the Persian ruler extended beyond matters of religion, the officer added. The commission for the Temple restoration had been granted to Sheshbazzar, a son of the beloved king Jehoiachin who had died in Babylon during the reign of Nabonidus. This Davidic prince of the blood had been designated Governor of Jerusalem by Cyrus and was thus to be the embodiment of Persian authority in the ancient capital of Judah. And why should the Persian king wish to do so grand a thing? It was in the nature of Cyrus' treatment of all his peoples, the soldier assured Jerusalem's Jews. The futility of suppressing racial and ethnic hopes had been demonstrated by the ugly histories of both Assyria and Babylon; but this was to be a new order. Persia would prosper and thrive as its people, benevolently yet firmly embraced by the rule from Pasargadae, found fulfillment in their own hopes and ideals. In return for his liberality, Cyrus requested of his peoples— Jerusalem among them —only their unqualified fidelity.

The Persian commander did not say so, but Cyrus had a special reason for wanting a secure and loyal Jerusalem. The imperial frontiers now extended to the borders of Egypt whose warriors, aside from those of the fierce Greeks, posed the greatest threat to the integrity of the empire's western flank. Since the brief clash of arms between Nebuchadrezzar and Pharaoh Amasis in 568, a weakened Egypt had been largely concerned with domestic matters and with her neighbors to the west and to the south. Meanwhile the Babylonians had been content to allow the Nile to irrigate an undisturbed civilization along its banks. But Cyrus' vision of Persia's destiny included a design upon the ancient kingdom beyond the Red Sea, and important to Egypt's submission would be the firm allegiance to the Persian court of Jerusalem, a likely staging area for any Egyptian adventure. If there were any better way of securing that loyalty than through the cooperation of a Davidic prince, sustained by the weight of Persian arms, Cyrus could not think what it might be.

The tall Jewish farmer, leaving his plow nose down in its furrow, had by now begun to lead his oxen home. In the total darkness, tempered ever so slightly by a full moon which lurked yet behind the eastern hills, the peasant had no difficulty in picking his way over a terrain whose every contour had been rendered familiar by years of work upon it. And within a very few minutes he would, with the unneeded aid of a bituminous torch, fodder the animals and pen them for the night. But as he walked in the lead of his beasts he continued lost in thought, his mind divided by conflicting emotions. The simple mention of the name of Sheshbazzar had caused certain sentinels within his soul to stand erect. For fifty years no member of the house of David had physically occupied Jerusalem's throne, yet the loyalty of the city to her monarch had refused to crumble with the devastated walls, and, for as long as King

Jehoiachin lived in his comfortable Babylonian confinement, many among Jerusalem's citizens counted him their king.

It was more than political loyalty; it was part of that ancient mystique which bound the Hebrew people to their God. The Davidic king had ruled in the Jerusalem of old as the agent of God himself, the divine deputy who was not simply responsible to God for the conduct of the nation's affairs, but who was also responsible to the people as the Deity's principal servant. Only as the king was faithful to the statutes and ordinances of God—so ran the lessons of the Great History—could spiritual loyalty and material prosperity be attained by the nation at large. It was therefore to be expected that the news that Cyrus was installing a Davidic prince to be the administrator of the city's affairs would kindle bonfires of hope in many a Jerusalemite's breast. And the lanky farmer's own imagination raced in trajectories of delight as he assured himself that the strong young man he had seen cantering beside the Persian cavalry officer was the royal prince.

Yet the plowman's joy was dampened by a disquieting fear. Like many of Jerusalem's inhabitants, his status and function in life rested on foundations firmly set atop the ruins of the old regime. This very land, for instance, which provided his livelihood and on which he had built his home was his by no title or deed. True, his father had worked it before him, but the senior farmer had merely appropriated it from previous owners who had disappeared after the second collapse of the city in 587. No one knew what had become of them, whether they had been killed or carried into exile. What if they or their heirs should now appear among Sheshbazzar's company to reclaim their farm? Where then would he go and how would he earn his bread? Shooing his animals into their enclosure, he whacked their hindquarters more vigorously than usual and knew that his reservations about the new arrivals from Babylon were shared by many within the city proper, a number of whose stakes were vastly larger than his own.

Sheshbazzar Enters Jerusalem[32]

When Cyrus' decree was read to the Jews in Babylon only shortly before it was declaimed in Jerusalem, it had fallen upon ears whose owners were no more of one mind than their kinsmen in Judah. The response to this gesture of Cyrus' good will fell into categories which were measurable by the degree to which a given Jewish family had come to terms with Babylonian life. Those whom comfort and prosperity had flushed with a sense of belonging in the Mesopotamian heartland—and these were by far the majority of the exiles—were indifferent to Cyrus' benevolence.

But those relative few who, by virtue of their alienation from Babylonian affairs, or who, because of the urgings of the Babylonian Isaiah or for other reasons, cherished the restoration of Jerusalem—these responded to the Persian overture and joined themselves to Sheshbazzar's company.

If Cyrus had expected a more eager reaction by Babylon's Jews, he expressed no dismay, and the imperial authorities exerted no pressure upon the exiles who opted to remain in Mesopotamia, many of them now as affluent as their Babylonian former masters, except to insist upon their help in defraying the costs of the pilgrims' journey. As for their own contribution, the Persians restored, as promised, the looted Temple treasures, they further sweetened the financial accounts of Sheshbazzar, and for protection in the barely subdued western fringes of their empire, they threw in a platoon of cavalry. Thus fortified, Sheshbazzar left Babylon in the company of perhaps two to three hundred other Jews in the spring of 538 and followed the well beaten caravan route from Babylon to Palestine, climbing up the valley of the Euphrates, then descending the Great Rift down through Damascus to Jerusalem.

The arrival of this caravan in the City of David was by no means in the nature of a triumphal entry. Sheshbazzar's royal blood plus the imposing presence of the Persian military insured that the protocol was courteous enough, and the formalities which the local Jewish leaders observed toward the prince and his company were reinforced by scenes of genuine popular emotion as many of Jerusalem's Jews, whose lives were greyed over by their shabby and unpleasant surroundings, remembered the glories of the dynasty of David and showered the prince with leaves and blossoms. But the reservations and fears which lurked in the city over the return of these possible rivals for land and prestige could be sensed by the more perceptive in Sheshbazzar's entourage, and, as food and lodgings had to be shared by the natives with the new arrivals, a few cross words fell forth even before the first sundown.

Nor did the physical appearance of the city contribute to elevating the spirits of the Jews from Babylon. Although they thought of their venture as a repatriation, in truth almost none of them had ever set foot inside Jerusalem before—only the most aged in their company, who had been born here, and a few of Sheshbazzar's immediate counselors, to whom the Babylonians had entrusted various missions here. And the sight of the ruined city, its walls ajumble, its Temple a blackened hulk, and its royal palace an enormous sandstone chaos, provided perhaps the first realistic inkling of the enormity of their task. As they dropped off to their first sleep in the city, their dreams must have been disturbed by the memory of the architectural grandeur and domestic comfort they had left behind.

JOSIAH
(640–609)

Moving force behind the Reformation of
621. Killed by the Egyptians at Megiddo
in 609. Succeeded by his son Jehoahaz.

JEHOAHAZ
(609)

Deposed by Pharaoh
Neco soon after his
father's death in fa-
vor' of his older half-
brother, Jehoiakim.

JEHOIAKIM
(609–598)

Ally of Egypt. Re-
volted against Baby-
lonian rule, but died
soon after. Succeeded
by his 18-year-old
son, Jehoiachin.

ZEDEKIAH
(597–587)

Last Davidic king
to rule over Judah
as king. Revolted
against Nebuchad-
rezzar in 588. Was
blinded and led in
chains to Babylon
after the fall of Jeru-
salem in 587.

JEHOIACHIN
(597)

Inherited his father's throne and rebellion, but quickly gave up to the Babylonians. Carried captive to Babylon where
he lived for many years and was treated
with some kindness. His throne passed to
his uncle Zedekiah.

SHESHBAZZAR
(SHENAZZAR)

First governor of Persian Jerusalem (538). Laid the foundation
for a new Temple. Fate unknown.

SHEALTIEL
ZERUBBABEL

Second governor of Persian Jeru-
salem (about 520). Completed the
Temple and became the object
of the intense royalist hopes of
Haggai, Zechariah, and the
Chronicler. Fate unknown.

THE LAST KINGS OF JUDAH

And those whose commitment to the resurrection of Jerusalem was equivocal must have endured the sting of second thoughts about their being here at all.

Sheshbazzar's Abortive Attempt at Temple Reconstruction

Sheshbazzar proceeded almost at once to implement the commission of Cyrus. Standing before the site of the ruined palace, the nearest approximation to a seat of government the city could boast, the Davidic prince, flanked by armed Persian troopers, declared anew Cyrus' authority over the old kingdom of Judah and read aloud his own credentials as governor. Shortly thereafter the prince addressed himself to the question of the new Temple. The first step was to rebuild the altar, a simple enough undertaking, and liturgically to purify it in order to render it fit for the ancient sacrificial ritual. And so, the rubble having been cleared from the site of the first altar and a new configuration of stones set carefully in its place, the appropriate priestly prayers were raised as the first flames in five decades jerked unevenly upward over this hallowed spot, spewing the pungent aroma of burned animal flesh into the air.

Then more rubble was cleared away and the foundations of the new building itself were laid. Wherever possible the outlines of the previous Temple were followed and heavy yellow stones were carefully laid in the receiving earth. Yet Sheshbazzar's budget was far less sumptuous than had been that of Solomon and many of the elegant features of the first Temple were omitted from the plans for the second, the result being that the new foundation was far less extensive than its predecessor.

> And when the builders laid the foundations of the temple of the LORD, the priests in their vestments came forward with trumpets, and the Levites, the sons of Asaph, with cymbals, to praise the LORD, according to the directions of David king of Israel; and they sang responsively, praising and giving thanks to the LORD,
> "For he is good,
>   for his steadfast love endures for
>   ever toward Israel."
> And all the people shouted with a great shout, when they praised the LORD, because the foundation of the house of the LORD was laid. But many of the priests and Levites and heads of fathers' houses, old men who had seen the first house, wept with a loud voice when they saw the foundation of this house being laid, though many shouted aloud for joy; so that the people could not distinguish the sound of the joyful shout from the sound of the people's weeping, for the people shouted with a great shout, and the sound was heard afar.
>
> (Ezra 3:10–13)

If certain of Jerusalem's Jews sheltered reservations about the return of the exiles, the Samaritans harbored even greater. And hardly had the mortar between the foundation stones hardened than they expressed themselves in the strongest possible terms. The enmity between Jerusalem and Samaria was deep and ancient, extending at least as far into the past as the tenth century when the northern city became a capital for those Hebrews who, by force of arms, had sloughed off the rule of the dynasty of David. Generations of intermittent warfare between the kinsmen of north and south followed this rupture in Israel's body politic, only to end in 722 when Assyrian armies crushed Samaria and, in scattered deportations, erased virtually all her peoples from the rolls of history. Only a remnant of Samaritans remained in Palestine, their blood polluted—so Jerusalem's Jews were fond of pointing out—by intermarriage with those gentiles whom the Assyrians had carted into Palestine to fill the population vacuum.

As family feuds are often the bitterest, so was the conflict between Jew and Samaritan especially sharp. With the collapse of Jerusalem and the exile of many of her people to Babylon, both antagonists stood upon the same shattered floor of humiliation. But now that Persia was taking steps, however limited, to restore the dignity of Jerusalem and that of her royal house, the Samaritans understandably feared domination by their deeply resented cousins. If the Temple were rebuilt, that might become the first terrible step in the reconstruction of the entire city and in Jerusalem's eventual arrogant sway over all of her immediate neighbors. Thus, after a Samaritan offer to join the Jews in the reconstruction of the Temple was rejected by Sheshbazzar—presumably because he suspected a ruse— the Samaritans vigorously appealed to Cyrus to have the work on the Temple halted.

The Persians were quite unprepared to force the issue. On the one hand, a secure military position in the area was high on their list of priorities, and for this reason alone, humanitarian concerns aside, they wanted a viable and prosperous Jerusalem. But on the other hand, prolonged civil strife in the region could easily undercut their own best interests by transforming the land into a cauldron of unrest. Thus the imperial authorities played for time by shunting the dispute into legal channels where, they hoped, the antagonists would exhaust their fury upon one another in the least destructive way.

> Then the people of the land [i.e., the Samaritans] discouraged the people of Judah, and made them afraid to build, and hired counselors against them to frustrate their purpose, all the days of Cyrus king of Persia, even until the reign of Darius king of Persia.
>
> (Ezra 4:4f.)

The upshot of this tangle was that the Temple, although functioning once more as a place of sacrifice, rose no higher than the level of the ground, while a frustrated Sheshbazzar retired into the wings of history from whence he was never again to emerge. And all the while men and women read the splendid and expansive promises of the Babylonian Isaiah: some hoped and expected, others scratched their scalps in bewilderment and doubt.

Zerubbabel Arrives in Jerusalem

When next we gain a glimpse of life in Jerusalem, it is because of larger events within the Persian Empire. In 529, nearly a decade after his proclamation to the Jews, Cyrus died, passing on to his son Cambyses a royal authority which was firmly in control of a vast and wealthy domain. Cambyses, who had inherited his father's thirst for power and his penchant for warfare, wasted no time in implementing a number of Cyrus' unfulfilled schemes and in extending the imperial horizons. Within four years the proud Egyptian kingdom was forcibly converted into a Persian satrapy and the Greek islands of Cyprus and Samos were assaulted and overcome.

Yet Cambyses was a far more cruel man than his father and was not above inflicting upon the people of his regions intense and needless suffering, the reports of his Egyptian campaign being especially unpleasant in this regard. And it was this cruel streak in Cambyses' nature which appears to have led him into a fatal mistake. The story, as we have it from King Darius' gigantic rock inscription at Behistun, is confused and its details not at all certain, but the matter seems to have gone something like this.[33] Cyrus had a younger son, named Bardiya, who held a special place in the popular esteem. Perhaps this was because he, unlike the older Cambyses, had been born after the merger of Persia and Media and was thus considered a crown prince of the united realm in a manner in which Cambyses could never have been. Or the affection of the people for Bardiya may have been stimulated by simple fear and disgust over Cambyses' harsh and oppressive ways. In any event, the new Persian monarch saw in Bardiya a threat to himself and ordered his brother secretly murdered; but for reasons quite unknown, he foolishly failed to exploit the crime. Instead of publicizing the death and passing it off as the result of an accident or of natural causes, he muted the entire affair.

Then in 522 while Cambyses was on a state visit to his new Egyptian provinces, an otherwise unknown holy man, Gaumata, who must somehow have discovered the secret of Bardiya's murder, began to travel through the cities and towns of the empire claiming to be the slain prince

Figure 34. Head of Darius.
Detail from the Behistun Rock.

and expressing strong pretensions to the throne. Within weeks Gaumata had raised a large army and Cambyses, hastily putting his own forces in order, found himself engaged in a desperate fight for his kingdom. In the midst of this struggle Cambyses died (whether by his own hand or that of someone else is unclear) and, as he had no natural heir, his death served only to intensify the civil disorder, several claimants to the throne falling upon Gaumata and upon one another in the contest for power.[34] Ultimately it was Darius, a cousin of Cambyses, who destroyed his rivals, seized the royal authority, and began the painstaking task of restoring public order. As Darius I he was to become one of Persia's most successful monarchs, for, during the nearly forty years of his rule, Persian arms pushed into Libya and into the lands of modern India, and one expedition into Europe even succeeded in fighting its way across the Danube.

This deep unrest throughout the Persian Empire seems profoundly to have affected the tiny Jewish colony in Jerusalem, and once more the curtain is pulled back and we see, although imperfectly, a series of impassioned events. After Darius had been proclaimed king, but well before he succeeded in supressing all rival aspirants to the throne, he appointed a new governor for Jerusalem. According to our best information, this occurred in 520, at least fifteen years after the last known activity of Sheshbazzar. The new governor was Zerubbabel, the son of a brother of Sheshbazzar, and thus a grandson of the late Judean king Jehoiachin. Zerubbabel's commission from Darius was the result of the Persian monarch's effort to bring stability to the restless imperial provinces, and in choosing another Davidic prince to administer Jerusalem he was doubtless motivated by considerations similar to those which had resulted in Sheshbazzar's earlier elevation to the same authority. Arriving with Zerubbabel was a member of the Jewish priestly class, Jeshua, whose ancestors had served in the Temple of Solomon and who was now appointed high priest. Also with the new governor there came from Babylon several thousand fresh Jewish emigres, persons for whom life in Mesopotamia seemed, in the present political scramble, not nearly so promising as it had in the rosier climate two decades before.

But if Darius' commission to Zerubbabel was accompanied by the belief that the presence of a new royal prince would have a tranquil and pacific effect upon the people, his judgment could not have been wider of the mark. The antipathy of the Samaritans to the reconstruction of the city and the imperial upheaval boiling all around had the effect of pushing from the minds of Jerusalem's Jews any reservations about Zerubbabel similar to those with which Sheshbazzar had been greeted. And the arrival in Jerusalem of the new party from Babylon led by an heir to the Davidic throne was a spark for the rekindling of all the old Jewish nationalistic expectations. Indeed, to some within the city, all of the ingredients seemed available for a reestablishment of the ancient institutions not only of Temple but of monarchy as well. It was hoped that perhaps Zerubbabel, as a new Solomon, would rebuild the Sanctuary of God upon the foundation abandoned by Sheshbazzar and his followers. Then, with the chief priest Jeshua at his side, might he proclaim once more the ancient authority of his forefather David and, in the name of the God of Israel, rule over a new Judah, risen, like the phoenix, from the ashes of the old! There is no way of knowing to what extent Zerubbabel himself may have helped to press the grapes of this heady wine, but it is clear that, either with or without his approval, these intoxicating visions charged the spirits of some of his fellow Jews. What, from our vantage point at least, looks dangerously like a conspiracy against the Persian rule was afoot.

Zerubbabel had scarcely bathed the dust of the journey from his hands and face when he was accosted by one Haggai, who claimed to speak as a prophet of the Lord and who directed the attention of the new governor and that of the high priest to the fact that the Temple still lay in ruins while the people had busied themselves with building their own comfortable houses.[35] This constituted an affront to God, he insisted, who had responded to the spiritual indifference of the people by sending a drought upon the land.

> Because of my house that lies in ruins, while you busy yourselves each with his own house, therefore the heavens above you have withheld the dew, and the earth has witheld its produce.
>
> (Hag. 1:9–10)

Haggai strongly implied that such conditions would continue as long as the Temple lay unbuilt.

Whether Zerubbabel's commission from Darius included the authorization to resume work on Sheshbazzar's barely begun edifice of worship we do not know. But the prominence of the high priest Jeshua in the

Figure 35. Sculptures and Inscription at Behistun Which Describe
Darius' Ascent to the Persian Throne.

company of the freshly arrived Jews leads one to suspect that it did and that Haggai's appeals were urging precisely what the new Davidic governor himself intended to do. In any event, work on the Temple was soon begun under the oversight of Zerubbabel and Jeshua and progressed well enough that a month after he had first spoken to the new governor, Haggai's heightened enthusiasm called forth a second prophetic oracle.

The gist of his new message was that the present project may appear to be poor and shabby when compared to the glory of Solomon's splendid edifice. But the builders should not be discouraged, for God himself would presently direct international events in such a manner as would fill this new Temple with dazzling beauty. Haggai is not specific as to precisely what events are to come to pass, but against the background of upheaval within the empire a bonanza is clearly in store for Jerusalem and its new Temple.

> I will shake all nations, so that the treasures of all nations shall come in, and I will fill this house with splendor, says the LORD of hosts.
>
> (Hag. 2:7)

Solomon's Temple is recalled.

> The latter splendor of this house shall be greater than the former, says the LORD of hosts; and in this place I will give prosperity.
>
> (Hag. 2:9)

And then in an electrifying series of words Haggai elevates the level of his prophetic discourse. No longer is the rebuilding of the Temple the object of his concern, but the reestablishment of the monarchy, specifically the enthronement of the present embodiment of the house of David, Zerubbabel. In a final oracle directed at Zerubbabel alone, Haggai proclaims these words from God:

> Speak to Zerubbabel, governor of Judah, saying, I am about to shake the heavens and the earth, and to overthrow the throne of kingdoms; I am about to destroy the strength of the kingdoms of the nations, and overthrow the chariots and their riders; and the horses and their riders shall go down, every one by the sword of his fellow. On that day, says the LORD of hosts, I will take you, O Zerubbabel my servant, the son of Shealtiel, says the LORD, and make you like a signet ring; for I have chosen you, says the LORD of hosts.
>
> (Hag. 2:20–23; cf. Jer. 22:24)

No one steeped in the events of recent years or familiar with the Jewish prophetic heritage could possibly be deaf to the tough import of Haggai's declaration: God would not be pleased until the Temple was restored and until a descendant of David sat upon his ancestor's throne as the deputy of the Lord.

Zechariah Prophesies Concerning Temple and Monarchy

Building the Temple and inaugurating anew the worship of God according to all of Israel's ancient rubrics was only a part of the responsibility Zerubbabel now found upon his hands. Of primary concern to his Persian masters and more to the nature of his office was the peaceful reintegration of the land to Darius, the coordination of those imperial affairs which impinged upon Jerusalem with the larger political purposes of the new royal regime, and the adjudication of local disputes such as the vexing Samaritan question. That such services were needed in this time of military turmoil and bureaucratic confusion within the empire is highlighted by the fact that the new governor's role in the Temple building scheme was quickly challenged, not as before by the Samaritans, but by his own Persian superior, the governor of the province "Beyond the River" (that is, west of the Euphrates) in whose larger jurisdiction Jerusalem lay (Ezra 5:3f.). Several weeks of charged confrontation ensued. Only after an appeal to the imperial court resulted in the recovery from the archives of the summer palace at Ecbatana of a copy of Cyrus' decree was the regional administration mollified and work on the Temple allowed to continue.

It may have been this effort at Persian intervention which summoned a second prophetic figure to thrust himself upon the scene of events. Haggai had unaccountably retired when, two months after his final recorded oracle, Zechariah took up the impassioned monologue. By this time the Persian military and political distress, which Haggai had seen as God's way of giving birth to a new Davidic monarchy, was beginning to be quelled and Darius was gaining control over an empire settling down to business as usual (Hag. 2:6–9; 21–23). "We have patrolled the earth," the angel of Zechariah's vision reports, "and all the earth remains at rest" (Zech. 1:11). Did this mean that Haggai had been wrong in seeing the hand of God at work in the Persian civil disturbances or in urging the reestablishment of monarchy and Temple? By no means! Appearances to the contrary, the enemies of the Jews would yet be discomforted and Jerusalem and her environs would flourish.

> Cry again, Thus says the LORD of hosts: My cities shall again overflow with prosperity, and the LORD will again comfort Zion and again choose Jerusalem.
>
> (Zech. 1:17)

Jeshua and Zerubbabel are as prominent in the oracles of Zechariah as they had been in those of Haggai. Yet, of the two, it is Zerubbabel who is singled out in a special way. Like David, he will conduct himself with divine authority.

Figure 36. Darius Receives His Captives. Carving on the Behistun Rock.

This is the word of the LORD to Zerubbabel: Not by might, nor by power, but by my Spirit, says the LORD of hosts.

(Zech. 4:6)

Like Solomon, he will build the Temple.

The hands of Zerubbabel have laid the foundations of this house; his hands shall also complete it.

(Zech. 4:9)

Indeed, Zerubbabel's work on the Temple will be consummated by his own coronation as Judah's rightful king and, in a pun upon Zerubbabel's name (which means "branch" or "sprout from Babylon"), Zechariah affirms that this new David will soon sit as the regent of the Lord God upon Judah's ancient throne.

Thus says the LORD of hosts, "Behold, the man whose name is the Branch: for he shall grow up in his place, and he shall build the temple of the LORD. It is he who shall build the Temple of the LORD, and shall bear royal honor, and shall sit and rule upon his throne. And there there shall be a priest beside his throne, and peaceful understanding shall be between them both."[36]

(Zech. 6:12f.)

A final series of oracles by Zechariah is dated in the ninth month of Darius' fourth regnal year, that is, 518 B.C. By now the work of Zerubbabel and his followers upon the Temple had been in progress more than two years. It seems to have progressed satisfactorily enough that Zechariah was encouraged to paint for his listeners a series of verbal portraits of the quality of life which must prevail in the new community where God would meet his people in the worship of the Temple, and where he would guide their lives through the instrument of the faithful Davidic king.

> These are the things that you shall do: Speak the truth to one another, render in your gates judgments that are true and make for peace, do not devise evil in your hearts against one another, and love no false oath, for all these things I hate, says the LORD.
>
> (Zech. 8:16f.)

The political security, financial wealth, and moral purity that will prevail in the restored Davidic kingdom will prove so attractive that

> in those days ten men from the nations of every tongue shall take hold of the robe of a Jew, saying, "Let us go with you, for we have heard that God is with you."
>
> (Zech. 8:23)

The Chronicler's History[37]

Figure 37. Fragment of a Glass Bowl Found Near Rome Bearing a Likeness of the Jerusalem Temple. From the Third or Fourth Century, A.D.

At about the time the walls of the new Temple were lifting their simple elegance into Jerusalem's skyline, there was deposited among the priestly and scribal archives, still stored with the returned Temple treasures in a nearby house, a new history of God's dealings with his people. Its author, himself a priest, had constructed with deliberate and reverential precision a fresh description of Israel's national experience and of her repeated confrontation by her God. Those who came across the new scroll in the city's literary repository knew without reading it what essential convictions its coiled sheets contained, for they had listened on many occasions to its lessons read aloud in public worship. Often in informal meetings for prayer and devotion, but more frequently on those grander occasions of praise beside the stunted Temple walls where vested priests intoned their chants and altar fires burned, the writer of this narrative or one of his associates would recite its urgent imperatives.

These new Chronicles had lessons, indeed, to tell. Like the stately Priestly History, sired in exile, the freshly inked narratives were committed to the crucial place in Israel's life of the ancient liturgy of worship, to those laws upon which that liturgy was based, and to the priestly personnel who supervised it. But Chronicles also shared a striking kinship to that Great History so closely linked to the Reformation of Josiah. Like this earlier narrative of Israel's life, Chronicles was profoundly concerned over the role of monarchy in the life of the people of God and in the relationship between the spiritual integrity of that institution and the status before God of the nation. Indeed, the Chronicler often wrote with a copy of the Great History before him, a method betrayed by the presence in his work of passages identical to those in the older narrative—frequently down to the last *waw* and *yodh*! In certain respects Chronicles formed a commentary upon the Great History, for at points its author assumed that his readers had learned the tales of the senior document and were conversant with its pointed spiritual maxims. But in other ways the new history set out to chart fresh paths.

In keeping with his keen interest in the Davidic monarchy, the Chronicler began his narrative with an account of the downfall of the unlamented King Saul and of the accession to the throne of the young warrior who was to become the father of Judah's kings. But the David who is portrayed on the pages of the new history is a figure larger than life, for removed are all of those sordid and untidy events of his reign, such as his unprincipled affair with Bathsheba and the harem intrigue which stained his declining days. Rather, the David of Chronicles is a virtually flawless monarch whose concern for liturgy and worship leads him to preside over the preparation for the building of the Temple, even to the procurement of cedar timbers from the King of Tyre and of the gold and silver treasures which are to grace the Temple's interior, acts which in the Great History had been attributed to Solomon (1 Chron. 22:3f.; 2 Chron. 2:3; cf. 1 Kings 5). Chronicles even reported that David had been entrusted with the actual blueprints of the Temple building "from the hand of God" (1 Chron. 28:19). And as a final, decisive act of state, David urged upon the people and upon his son Solomon that they keep faith with God and with David himself by finishing the project which he had so auspiciously begun.

Solomon proved faithful to the commission from his father and from God, as whose representative David had spoken, and the Temple was soon finished and dedicated, the Chronicler describing these events in extended passages borrowed almost totally from the Great History. Then the skein of the life of the people of God is unrolled right up to the time of the terrible collapse of Jerusalem under Zedekiah, and its quality is tested at every point by reference to the people's degree of faithfulness to the liturgy of the Temple and to the word of the Lord as spoken by the mouths of God's prophets. The conduct of affairs in the rebellious Northern Kingdom, followed so closely by the Great History, is dismissed by the Chronicler on the grounds that, because of Samaria's rejection of the ordinances of the Jerusalem Temple and her failure to heed the prophet's word, she had cut herself off from the life of God's people.

Yet Judah herself had ultimately failed the same test. Although David's sons upon Judah's throne had produced such examples of piety and faithfulness as Jehoshaphat, Hezekiah, and Josiah, many of the Davidic kings had proved unworthy of their holy responsibilities, had ignored the good offices of Temple worship, and had turned a deaf ear to the prophetic voice. The Chronicler's indictment of Judah's last king became an interpretation of the nation's entire tragic drama by which she had beat herself to pieces upon the shoals of her own impiety and faithlessness.

> [Zedekiah] stiffened his neck and hardened his heart against turning to the LORD, the God of Israel. All the leading priests and the people likewise were exceedingly unfaithful, following all the abominations of the nations; and they polluted the house of the LORD which he had hallowed in Jerusalem.
>
> The LORD, the God of their fathers, sent persistently to them by his messengers, because he had compassion on his people and on his dwelling place; but they kept mocking the messengers of God, despising his words, and scoffing at his prophets, till the wrath of the Lord rose against his people, till there was no remedy.
>
> Therefore he brought up against them the king of the Chaldeans. . . .
> (2 Chron. 36:13b–17a)

The Chronicler, however, had not preached these sermons to the people worshipping in the shadow of the Temple's newly-risen walls simply in order to probe old wounds. The present task was one of extreme difficulty and of compelling urgency. In the face of grumbling by the Samaritans and harassment from the Persian authorities, and under the heavy burden of expenditures such a project imposed upon a people of modest means, the temptation to abandon the reconstruction of the Temple was surely a persistent one. But God's will must be done! The Sanctuary must be completed! To do otherwise would be to repeat the terrible sins of old! And so those words from the mouth of David for Solomon now became God's own clarion to the present generation.

Now set your mind and heart to seek the LORD your God. Arise and
build the sanctuary of the LORD God, so that the ark of the covenant of
the LORD and the holy vessels of God may be brought into a house built
for the name of the LORD.

(1 Chron. 22:19)

And you, Solomon my son, . . . take heed now, for the LORD has chosen
you to build a house for the sanctuary; be strong, and do it.

(1 Chron. 28:9f.)

Then David said to Solomon his son, "Be strong and of good courage,
and do it. Fear not, be not dismayed; for the LORD God, even my God, is
with you. He will not fail you or forsake you, until all the work for the
service of the house of the LORD is finished.

(1 Chron. 28:20)

Yet the Chronicler's understanding of God's will for Jerusalem envisioned more than a new Temple edifice. Only as Temple worship was
coupled to obedience to the divine words of the prophets and to the
authority of the Davidic king could God's people be exposed to his mul-
tiple means of grace and could the nation express its own fidelity to her
sovereign Lord. The prophetic word was now abroad in the land, through
the efforts of Haggai, Zechariah, and perhaps others; and if all went as
it should, the Temple would soon be restored. That left only the vacant
chair of David to be filled. And to that end the Chronicler's impassioned
pleas were directed.

The word of the LORD came to me saying, ". . . Behold, a son shall be
born to you; . . . He shall build a house for my name. He shall be my
son, and I will be his father, and I will establish his royal throne in
Israel for ever." Now, my son, the LORD be with you, so that you may
succeed in building the house of the LORD your God, as he has spoken
concerning you. Only, may the LORD grant you discretion and understanding, that when he gives you charge over Israel you may keep the
law of the LORD your God. Then you will prosper if you are careful to
observe the statutes and the ordinances which the LORD commanded
Moses for Israel. Be strong, and of good courage. Fear not; be not dismayed . . . Arise and be doing! The LORD be with you!

(1 Chron. 22:8f.)

No one else in Israel's long history had stressed so vigorously the links
between the Davidic king and the worship within the Temple, and
the Chronicler's lessons were not lost upon his hearers and readers. God
had now furnished his people with a scion of David to erect the House
of God, and the people must respond by hearing the prophetic word,
raising the Sacred Building, and crowning Zerubbabel king!

The Collapse of Royalist Hopes

On the twelfth of March, 515, five labored years after the arrival in
Jerusalem of Zerubbabel and nearly a quarter century following the

proclamation of Cyrus, the final stone of the Temple was gingerly set in its place amid scenes of extended jubilation. And shortly thereafter the new sanctuary was consecrated to the worship of God and made the focus of such a Passover festival as had seldom before been seen.

> And the people of Israel, the priests and the Levites, and the rest of the returned exiles, celebrated the dedication of this house of God with joy. They offered at the dedication of this house of God one hundred bulls, two hundred rams, four hundred lambs, and as a sin offering for all Israel twelve he-goats, according to the number of the tribes of Israel. And they set the priests in their divisions and the Levites in their courses, for the service of God at Jerusalem, as it is written in the book of Moses.
>
> On the fourteenth day of the first month the returned exiles kept the passover. For the priests and the Levites had purified themselves together; all of them were clean. So they killed the passover lamb for all the returned exiles, for their fellow priests, and for themselves; it was eaten by the people of Israel who had returned from exile, and also by every one who had joined them and separated himself from the pollutions of the peoples of the land to worship the LORD, the God of Israel. And they kept the feast of the unleavened bread seven days with joy. . . .
>
> (Ezra 6:16–22)

The jubilation was well fueled. The creamy stones of the building, glistening in the hot Palestinian sun before the eyes of the people, were a tangible proof that God, their God, was with them and that all of the prophetic promises were coming true. The rich robes of the priests, flecked with gold and jewels, and the costly sacred objects from the old Temple, carried with grandest pomp into the new, formed a dazzling reminder that soon the treasures of the nations would pour into the coffers of the Temple. And, as Jeshua and his priests were inaugurated into their official responsibilities in the Temple routine, tasks restored after three quarters of a century of disuse, many a glance was cast upon Zerubbabel, for the next inauguration would be his. At that time, clad in the regal splendor of the Davidic king, he would receive from Jeshua the anointing of holy oil, as did David from Zadok, and, resting upon the twin foundations of monarchy and cult, the people of God would stride confidently into a future in which civilized life stood ordered and arranged by a God whom men could know only as they were taught by the Jews.

Yet no sooner has this effervescence overflowed than a mighty hush falls upon the biblical record. Suddenly we hear no more of the peppery urgings of Haggai and Zechariah, nor do we glean from the Chronicler any fresh harvest of hope fulfilled. And as for the Book of Ezra, which has guided us through these terrible years of hardship and sacrifice, it shows us the joy over the completed Temple and then abandons us on the edge of an abyss, a crevice into which no glimmer of light has penetrated. Zerubbabel's name is never raised again, and those high expectations surrounding his person disappear like the mists of a September morning. A trap door is sprung upon the stage of Judah's life into which men and the hopes surrounding them are swallowed without a trace.

We do not have any evidence that Zerubbabel himself ever gave shelter to the aspirations of others that he should become king. And it may be that, following the completion of the Temple, he simply fulfilled his term as Jerusalem's governor and then retired into quiet anonymity, leaving his zealous supporters clutching a bag of empty dreams. But other possibilities linger to haunt us. That a prince of the blood would turn a deaf ear to the voices of those who wished to hand him a throne would be an unusual, although not singular, circumstance. And perhaps Zerubbabel did relent to the demands of Haggai and Zechariah and to the historically shaped urgings of the Chronicler by making certain moves toward a royalist restoration, only to suffer the full weight of the Persian wrath.

We shall probably never be sure. One certainty, however, which does emerge out of the heavy air of the centuries is that, contrary to the white-hot dreams of many in the restored city, no son of David ever again warms the throne of his great ancestor or presides in splendor over a city which has become the envy of mankind.

Ezra, Nehemiah, and After[38]

Two small corridors of light are admitted into the arena of Jerusalem's life before a prolonged and stubborn darkness sets in. In 458 Zerubbabel's Temple, now in its second half-century of life, is again the object of Persian munificence when a Jewish priest from Babylon, Ezra, arrives in the city with gold and silver sent by the imperial government and by private Jewish citizens of Mesopotamia (Ezra 7:25f.). He also comes armed with civil authority from the Persians which entitles him to make certain judicial appointments for the enforcement of imperial laws and which also authorizes him to see to the implementation of Jewish priestly statutes in the city proper. Ezra's initial energies are directed to the expulsion of non-Jewish partners of the community's biracial marriages, a matter which he presses by preaching a vigorous outdoor sermon in a driving rain (Ezra 10:9f.). Then, several weeks later, the priest stands in a public square upon a small wooden pulpit especially constructed for the occasion and from early morning until noon he reads to the people from "the Book of the Law of Moses," (perhaps some form of the Priestly History) and the next day leads them in the restoration of the ancient harvest ritual, the Feast of Booths (Neh. 8).

A second embassy from the Persian court arrived in the following decade. Led by Nehemiah, a Jew in the employment of Persian King

Artaxerxes I, and provided with muscle by the presence of imperial cavalrymen, this deputation of the year 445 was commissioned to rebuild Jerusalem's still blackened walls at a time when the unprotected city was the object of threats and intimidation from her neighbors (Neh. 1f.). Nehemiah, who thwarted his enemies by his famous nocturnal survey of the devastated walls and by arming his workers, succeeded in erecting the city's fortifications a century and a half after their destruction by Nebuchadrezzar. Like Ezra, he demanded of the people a number of measures—the keeping of the Sabbath and (again!) the expulsion of non-Jewish wives—to preserve the sanctity of the priestly law. And his memoirs, preserved in the biblical book which bears his name, close his own account of his days in Jerusalem with a simple and pious exhortation which recalls the previously quoted building inscription of Nebuchadrezzar: "Remember me, O my God, for good" (Neh. 13:31).

We are only imperfectly aware of Jerusalem's fortunes over the next centuries. The city remained in the possession of the Persian kings, loyally as best we know, until the grand kingdom which Cyrus had forged fell to the first of Europe's builders of empire, Alexander of Macedon, remembered by history as "the Great." But the Greek habits and ideals which followed the march of Alexander's phalanxes came to clash with conservative Jewish ways, and a century and a half after the Macedonian's death Jerusalem revolted against his Seleucid successors and, under the brilliant sons of Mattathias, a priest of the village of Modin, established an independence which was to stand for more than six decades. The city made no known effort to restore the house of David during those brave days, but instead entrusted the affairs of state to this capable priestly family (the Maccabees). Yet not even Jewish priests were a match for the legions of Rome, and in 63 B.C. the City of David fell to the advancing columns of Pompey. The last glow of Jewish independence was extinguished, not to flame again until modern times.

During all of these years Zerubbabel's Temple stood stoutly, if not magnificently, upon the site of Solomon's original building and offered to the people a place of worship and, occasionally, of physical protection as well. No account of its appearance has come down to us, but it is doubtful if anyone praised its beauty. It was, in fact, the very plainness of the structure which caused its destruction by Herod. The puppet ruler of Roman Judea, as a part of his scheme to awe the subjects who loathed him, built a third and—as it turned out—last Temple for the worship in Jerusalem of the God of Israel, a structure which itself fell victim to conflagration with which the Romans crushed the Jewish revolt of 70 A.D.

Two decades after Zerubbabel's Sanctuary, raised among such lofty expectations, was pulled to the ground, Jesus of Nazareth was born.[39]

V.

A REFLECTION

Have you not known? Have you not heard?
The Lord is the everlasting God,
*   the Creator of the ends of the earth.*
He does not faint or grow weary,
*   his understanding is unsearchable.*
He gives power to the faint,
*   and to him who has no might he*
*   increases strength.*
Even youths shall faint and be weary,
*   and young men shall fall exhausted;*
but they who wait for the Lord shall
*   renew their strength,*
*   they shall mount up with wings like*
*   eagles,*
they shall run and not be weary,
*   they shall walk and not faint.*

—Isaiah 40:28–31

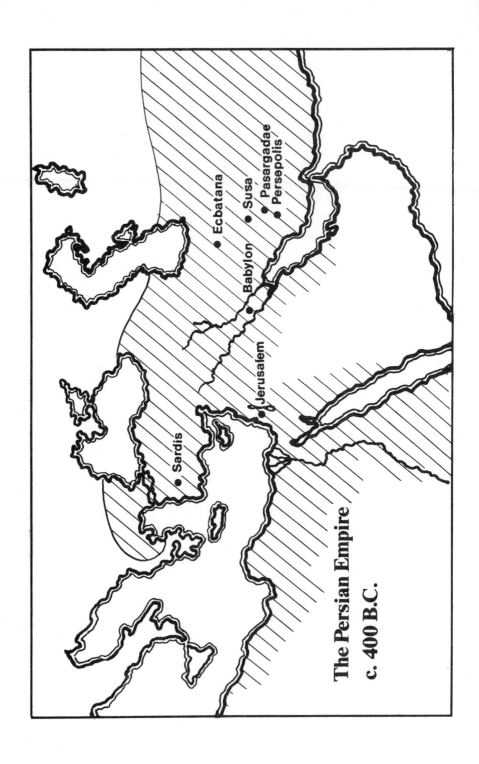

The Persian Empire
c. 400 B.C.

Sardis

Ecbatana

Babylon

Jerusalem

Susa
Pasargadae
Persepolis

Chapter Seven

Whither shall I go from thy Spirit?
Or whither whall I flee from thy presence?
If I ascend to heaven, thou art there!
If I make my bed in Sheol, thou art there!
If I take the wings of the morning
and dwell in the uttermost parts of the sea,
even there thy hand shall lead me,
and thy right hand shall hold me.
If I say, "Let only darkness cover me,
and the light about me be night,"
even the darkness is not dark to thee,
the night is as bright as day;
for darkness is as light with thee.

—Psalm 139:7–12

The man shifted his feet and sank his plump, well fed body farther down into the great overstuffed chair which, for its part, readily swallowed this additional bulk. His pink, good natured cheeks framed a broad smile through which friendly, tobacco stained teeth shimmered dully and out of which a cigar dangled like an inverted exclamation point. He discharged a cloud of grey smoke into the air and then, reaching forward, accepted the coffee offered by our host. His lips released the dark Havana long enough to test the scalding beverage and to permit him to say, "The sad truth is that there's no one in charge. I only wish there were, but there isn't. No one." In went the cigar once more, but popped out briefly as an afterthought surfaced: "Not in this world, at least." The man grinned more broadly than before and winked pleasantly at his interlocutors.

This observation was the climax to an after-dinner discussion which had ranged over a number of those political and social issues which have in recent years rendered human life and happiness so precarious. Its author was a distinguished lecturer in history who had animated the conversation all evening by his frequent references to events of the past and by his imaginative—sometimes frightful—scenarios for the future. This final declaration, although made in all good humor, came across to his listeners as a plaintive cry of resignation that, no matter how hard mankind might try to program his own future in constructive and beneficial ways, the human adventure was, at bottom, a capricious and sometimes meaningless experience.

Had this learned and likeable man lived as a Jew in Jerusalem or in Babylon in the sixth century B.C., he would certainly have had many bricks with which to build a house of pessimism. "Our bones are dried up, and our hope is lost; we are clean cut off" (Ezek. 37:11), was the lament of the exiles. And if God seems distant, or hostile, or non-existent to many in our own time, he seemed just as much so to the Jews of the exile. Indeed, this was the challenge which Jeremiah and, after him, Ezekiel and the Babylonian Isaiah, rose to meet with their declaration that, in spite of many appearances to the contrary, God is in control of the affairs of men and of nations and is shaping human history according to his will. Not that men and women do not often act in ways which thwart that will and deny God's sovereign lordship—Judah's own sinful past constituted the most pointed example that they do. But the ignorance and waywardness of mankind notwithstanding, the world is never out of God's control, nor is it capable of wrenching itself irremediably from his compassionate and benevolent hand.

Our own era is one which has seen a vast amount of suffering and despair and which has experienced even more disorientation and loss of meaning than that deposited upon the Jews of the sixth century B.C. Two global wars and a multitude of local ones, the emergence of political tyrannies as ruthless as they are powerful, the abandonment of many traditional values in favor of revolutionary styles of life and relationship have resulted in a profound sensation of misdirection and futility. The despondent cry of Rolf Hochhuth's Jewess in the boxcar to Auschwitz is the anguished voice of many in our own century.

> No hope, beloved, that you will ever find me.
> Cold, God is cold as the pomp of San Giovanni's
> It's nothing to him that this woman next to me
> Will never bear her child, that I will never be yours.
> Cold, God is cold; my hands grow numb
> When I try to fold them to pray with.
> And the gods of the ancients are dead as their legends,
> Dead as the antique rubble in the Vatican museum,
> The morgue of art. Or else I would hope you would find me
> As Orpheus found Eurydice.[39]

In the face of all such appeals for meaning, the experience of Judah's exile and restoration stands as symbol. In spite of the suffering and alienation injected into life by the evil and waywardness of the human heart, God's promise is one of compassionate restoration of mankind, and his spirit is abroad to redeem and to renew both individual men and women and those human structures within which life must be lived.

Figure 38. Enamelled Tile from the Palace of the Persian Kings at Susa.

And at no time is the course of human history beyond his loving control, no matter how our own sinfulness or that of someone else imposed upon us makes difficult the effort to experience that control. God's promises are true and, in spite of frequent human intentions to the contrary, will be fulfilled.

> And you shall know that I am the LORD, when I open your graves, and raise you from your graves, O my people. And I will put my Spirit within you, and you shall live.
>
> (Ezek. 37:13f.)

This is the Gospel in its finest Old Testament flowering.

But having affirmed God's sovereign rule over history, the experience of exile and restoration underscores all too vividly that, when God's promises are fulfilled, it is frequently in ways which not even his most faithful people could have expected or anticipated, and perhaps in ways which, for the moment, cause it to appear that the promises have not been fulfilled at all. It seems clear that Haggai, Zechariah, and the Chronicler conceived of God's role in Jerusalem's life as that of the One who, having restored the people to the land, would then move on to the consummation of his redemptive activity by the rebuilding of the Temple, the coronation of Zerubbabel as the new Davidic king, and the flooding of the city with prosperity and good fortune. And in thinking in such terms, they were clearly relying upon the words of others, particularly Ezekiel and the Babylonian Isaiah, whose vision of God's redemptive power made ample room for monarchy and wealth. (Ezek. 34; Isa. 49:19f.) But as it turned out, that is not what happened at all. Although the Temple was rebuilt, Zerubbabel never became king, nor did the "treasure of all nations" glut a newly independent Jerusalem with riches (Hag. 2:7). Rather, for most of the period until her destruction by the Romans in 70 A.D., Jewish Jerusalem was the vassal of one or another of the great world powers, often impoverished, always conducting her Temple worship in Zerubbabel's unpretentious building or in Herod's misbegotten one. To be sure, the city lived, as did the faith of its inhabitants, but those who viewed the promises of restoration from exile in terms of a resurrection of the glory of the old Israel of David and Solomon were not to be sustained.

God's promises *were* fulfilled, but the Davidic king proved to be no grand and regal magistrate. He was instead a Galilean peasant whose charger was a donkey and whose courtiers were fishermen. His rule was to prove far more crucial for mankind than that of all other kings together, but not by virtue of the strength of David or the splendor of Solomon. His majesty was climaxed in his fulfillment of the vision of the Babylonian Isaiah concerning the Servant of the Lord who suffers for the sake of all mankind. And because of him men and women of virtually every nation on earth have looked to Jerusalem, not as the place to lay their silver and gold, but as that small stage on which the most important drama of human life was enacted: His death and resurrection. If the Babylonian Isaiah and the Chronicler and all the rest sensed what God was up to in a most imperfect and fragmented way, and if Jesus' own contemporaries were often blind to the larger meaning of his messianic service, we should express no amazement. The human expectation of what God will do or ought to do is rarely adequate, for the simple reason that the pigeonholes of the human brain cannot fully comprehend, nor can the tools of human language adequately convey, the size and shape of the mind of God. Thus when God does consummate his ideals for human life, we are inevitably surprised.

This is the reason why all of our detailed schemes of the future, so popular with many Christians, are of such doubtful value, even when they are extracted from Scripture itself, visions having to do with the Second Coming of Christ, the end of the world, and the like. No matter how deep our commitment to God's promises, nor how well rehearsed our knowledge of his ways, the Father of our Lord Jesus Christ, who refuses to be bound by any of the categories of human thought, is invariably a God of the most compassionate astonishment and wonder. And when all has been said and done, how could we even want him to be any other way?

For my thoughts are not your thoughts,
  neither are your ways my ways, says the LORD.
For as the heavens are higher than the earth,
  so are my ways higher than your ways
  and my thoughts than your thoughts.

For as the rain and snow come down from heaven,
  and returns not thither but water the earth,
making it bring forth and sprout,
  giving seed to the sower and bread to the eater,
so shall my word be that goes forth from my mouth;
  it shall not return to me empty,
but it shall accomplish that which I purpose,
  and prosper in the thing for which I sent it.
                                    (Isa. 55:8–11)

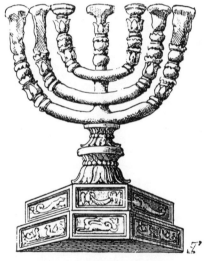

Figure 39. Candlesticks from the Jerusalem Temple. Reproduced on the Titus
Arch in Rome, a Monument Built to Commemorate
the Fall of Jerusalem in 70 A.D.

Appendix I:

Chronological Tables for the Years 640–500 B.C.

	EGYPT	ISRAEL	BABYLON
640		640?—Josiah's rule begins	
638			
636			
634	Period of relative weakness under Psammetichus I (663–609)	Judah grows less subservient to Assyrian domination	Assyria strong but declining under Ashurbanipal (668–627)
632			
630		Prophet Zephaniah active	
		629—Preliminary reforms under Josiah (?) (2 Chron. 34:3)	
628		627—Jeremiah begins his ministry	627—Ashurbanipal dies
626		625—Birth of Ezekiel (?)	626—Assyrians driven from Babylon by Nabopolassar

	EGYPT	ISRAEL	BABYLON
624			
622			
		621—Josiah's Reformation	
620			
618		First edition of the Great History	
616			
614			
612			612—Fall of Ninevah
610	610—Neco begins to rule Egypt		
		609—Josiah killed —Jehoahaz rules briefly —Jehoiakim ascends Judean throne as Egyptian vassal	
608			

	EGYPT	ISRAEL	BABYLON
606			
	605—Battle of Carchemish, Egyptians defeated		605—Carchemish —Nebuchadrezzar succeeds Nabopolassar
604		604—Jerusalem subjected to Babylonian authority	604—Ashkelon falls to Nebuchadnezzar
602			
	601—Neco defeats Nebuchadnezzar in battle	601—Jehoiakim revolts	601—Nebuchadrezzar loses control of southern Palestine to Egyptians
600			
598		598—Nebuchadrezzar marches upon Jerusalem	
		597—Jehoiachin succeeds Jehoiakim —Jerusalem surrenders to Babylonians, March 16, 597 —Zedekiah becomes king	597—Jehoiachin and many other Jews deported to Babylon
596			595—Revolt among Jews in Babylon
594	594—Neco dies, succeeded by Psammetichus II	594—conspiratorial meeting in Jerusalem involving Edom, Moab, Ammon, Tyre, Sidon	594—Babylonian Chronicle breaks off —Ezekiel's first oracle
592			
590			
	589—Apries (Hophra) begins to rule in Egypt		

	EGYPT	ISRAEL	BABYLON
588		588—Zedekiah revolts —Nebuchadrezzar invades Judah 587—Jerusalem falls	
586		—Blinded Zedekiah and many others to Babylon —Gedeliah killed —Jeremiah kidnapped to Egypt	586—Siege of Tyre begins
584			
582		582—A third deportation (?) (Jer. 52:30)	
580			
578		Second edition of the Great History "published," probably in Jerusalem	Jewish priests in Babylon engaged in codification of the Law
576			
574			
			573—Tyre falls to Nebuchadrezzar
572			
			571—Ezekiel's last prophecy (?) (Ezek. 29:17)

	EGYPT/PERSIA	ISRAEL	BABYLON
570	570—Amasis begins to rule Egypt		
568	568—Conflict with Babylon		568—Nebuchadrez-zar campaigns against Egypt
566			
564			
562		562—King Jehoia-chin, still a prisoner in Babylon, is elevated to the king's table	562—Nebuchad-rezzar dies —Amel-Marduk rules
560			560—Amel-Marduk overthrown in favor of Nergal-shar-usur
558			Priestly History in composition
556	556?—Cyrus attacks Astyages, king of Media		556—Nergal-shar-usur dies —Brief rule of Labashi-Marduk —Accession of
554			Nabonidus

	PERSIA	ISRAEL	BABYLON
552			
550	549—Cyrus defeats Astyages, unites kingdoms of Media and Persia		Nabonidus absent from Babylon for a number of years.
548	547—Cyrus defeats Croesus, king of Lydia		Belshazzar administers city's affairs
546			
544			Babylonian Isaiah active
542			
540			
	539—Cyrus takes Babylon		539—Babylon falls to Cyrus
538	538—Cyrus' decree concerning Jerusalem	538—Initial return of Jews under Sheshbazzar —Temple foundations laid	
536		—No further news of Sheshbazzar	

	PERSIA	ISRAEL	BABYLON
534			
532			
530	630—Cyrus dies —Succeeded by his son Cambyses		
528			
526			
	525—Cambyses conquerors Egypt		
524			
522	522—Bardiya's revolt 521—Darius assumes Persian throne		522—Babylon briefly revolts against Persian rule under self- styled Nebuch- adrezzar III
520		520—Zerubbabel to Jerusalem as governor —He and Joshua addressed by Haggai and Zechariah —Work begun on new Temple	
518			

	PERSIA	ISRAEL	BABYLON
516			
		515—New Temple finished and dedicated. No further reports of Zerubbabel	
514	513?—Darius crosses the Danube	—Early edition of 1 and 2 Chronicles "published"	
512			
510			
508			
	Darius actively expands Persia's frontiers		
506			
504			
502			
500			

Appendix II:

Index of Scripture References

Selected Bibliography

Abbreviations

AB   The Anchor Bible
BASOR   Bulletin of the American Schools of Oriental Research
IB   The Interpreter's Bible
IDB   The Interpreter's Dictionary of the Bible
JBL   Journal of Biblical Literature
OTL   The Old Testament Library

Ackroyd, Peter R. *Exile and Restoration.* OTL. Philadelphia: Westminster, 1968.
Bowman, Raymond A. "Introduction and Exegesis of Ezra and Nehemiah." IB, Vol. 3, pp. 515–819.
Bright, John. *A History of Israel.* OTL. Philadelphia; Westminster, 1959.
———. *Jeremiah.* AB 21. Garden City: Doubleday, 1965.
Burrows, Millar. "Jerusalem." IDB, vol. 2, pp. 843–66.
Comay, Joan. *The Temple of Jerusalem.* London: Widenfeld & Nicholson, 1975.
Cross, Frank M. "A Reconstruction of the Judean Restoration." JBL (94), March 1975, pp. 4–18.
Dalberg, B. T. "Sheshbazzar." IDB, Vol. 4, p. 325f.
———. "Zerubbabel." IDB, Vol. 4, p. 955f.
Dresden, M. J. "Darius." IDB, Vol. 1, p. 769f.
Eichrodt, Walter. *Ezekiel.* Translated by Cosslett Quin. OTL. Philadelphia: Westminster, 1970.
———. *Theology of the Old Testament.* Translated by J. A. Baker. OTL. Philadelphia: Westminster, 1961, 1967.
Finegan, Jack. *Light From the Ancient Past.* Princeton: Princeton University Press, 1946.
Freedman, David N. "The Chronicler's Purpose." Catholic Biblical Quarterly 22 (1961), pp. 436–42.
Ginsberg, H. L. "An Aramaic Contemporary of the Lachish Letters." Bulletin of the American Schools of Oriental Research, 111 (1948), pp. 24–27.
Gray, John. *I & II Kings.* Revised Edition. OTL. Philadelphia: Westminster, 1970.
Howie, C. G. "Ezekiel." IDB, Vol. 2, pp. 203–13.
Hyatt, J. Philip. "Introduction and Exegesis of Jeremiah." IB, Vol. 5, pp. 777–1141.
Kenyon, Kathleen M. *Jerusalem.* New York: McGraw-Hill, 1967.
McKenzie, John L. *Second Isaiah.* AB, Vol. 20. Garden City: Doubleday, 1968.
May, Herbert G. "Introduction and Exegesis of Ezekiel." IB, Vol. 6, pp. 41–338.
Muilenberg, James. "The History of the Religion of Israel." IB, Vol. 1, pp. 292–348.
Myers, Jacob M. *I Chronicles.* AB 12. Garden City: Doubleday, 1965.
———. *II Chronicles.* AB 13. Garden City: Doubleday, 1965.
———. *Ezra, Nehemiah* AB 14. Garden City: Doubleday, 1965.
Neil, W. "Haggai." IDB, Vol. 2, pp. 509–11.
———. "Zechariah, Book of." IDB, Vol. 4, pp. 943–47.

Newsome, James D. "Toward A New Understand of the Chronicler and His Purposes." JBL (94), June 1975, pp. 201–217.

North, Christopher R. "History." IDB, Vol. 2, pp. 607–12.

———. "Isaiah." IDB, Vol. 2, pp. 731–44.

———. *The Second Isaiah.* Oxford: The Clarendon Press, 1964.

———. "Servant of the Lord." IDB, Vol. 4, pp. 292–94.

———. *The Suffering Servant in Deutero-Isaiah.* London: Geoffrey Cumberlege (Oxford University Press), 1956.

Noth, Martin. *The History of Israel.* London: Adam and Charles Black, 1948.

———. *Leviticus.* Translated by J. E. Anderson. OTL. Philadelphia: Westminster, 1965.

———. *The Old Testament World.* Translated by Victor L. Gruhn. Philadelphia: Fortress, 1966.

Olmstead, A. T. *History of the Persian Empire.* Chicago: The University of Chicago Press, 1948, 1959.

Oppenheim, A. L. "Assyria and Babylonia." IDB, Vol. 1, pp. 262–304.

———. "Nabonidus." IDB, Vol. 3, p. 493f.

———. "Nebuchadnezzar." IDB, Vol. 3, p. 529f.

———. "Evil-Merodach." IDB, Vol. 2, p. 183.

Pfeiffer, R. H. "Ezra and Nehemiah." IDB. Vol. 2, pp. 215–19.

Pritchard, J. B., ed. *Ancient Near Eastern Texts Relating to the Old Testament.* Princeton: Princeton Univ. Press, 3rd ed., 1969.

von Rad, Gerhard. *Deuteronomy.* Translated by Dorothea Barton. OTL. Philadelphia: Westminster, 1966.

———. "Deuteronomy." IDB, Vol. 1, pp. 831–38.

———. *Genesis.* Translated by John Marks. Revised Edition. OTL. Philadelphia: Westminster, 1972.

Saggs, H. W. F. *The Greatness That Was Babylon.* London: Sidgwick and Jackson, 1962.

Sanders, J. A. "Exile." IDB, Vol. 2, pp. 186–88.

Scoggin, J. A. *Joshua.* Translated by R. A. Wilson. OTL. Philadelphia: Westminster, 1972.

Stinespring, W. F. "Temple." IDB, Vol. 4, pp. 534–60.

Thomas, D. W. "Introduction and Exegesis of Haggai." IB, Vol. 6, pp. 1037–1049.

———. "Introduction and Exegesis of Zechariah." IB, Vol. 6, pp. 1053–1114.

Westermann, Claus. *Isaiah 40–66.* Translated by David M. H. Stalker. OTL. Philadelphia: Westminster, 1969.

Wilson, J. W. "Neco." IDB, Vol. 3, p. 530f.

Wiseman, D. J. *Chronicles of the Chaldean Kings (626–556 B.C.) in the British Museum.* London: The Trustees of the British Museum, 1956.

Wright, G. E. "Introduction and Exegesis of Deuteronomy." IB, Vol. 2, pp. 311–537.

Notes

1. Our chief source of knowledge relative to the reign of Nebuchadrezzar is the baked clay tablets of the so-called "Babylonian Chronicle," a contemporary court history written in cuneiform and providing facts concerning each of Nebuchadrezzar's regnal years from his coronation in 605 B.C. until 595 B.C. After the latter date only one other tablet is extant, recording events during the years 557–556 when one of the successors of Nebuchadrezzar, Nergal-shar-usur, sat upon Babylon's throne. As mentioned in the text, there is reason to believe that the Chronicle originally dealt not only with the entire rule of Nebuchadrezzar (as well as with that of his father, Nabopolassar), but with much more of the later history of the New Babylonian Empire as well. The hope must be cherished that someday more of this important record will come to light, thus diminishing our ignorance of the activities of Nebuchadrezzar and of conditions in Babylon during the Jewish exile.

A translation of the existing tablets has been published, accompanied by a valuable commentary, in D. J. Wiseman, *Chronicles of the Chaldean Kings (626–556) in the British Museum* (London: Trustees of the British Museum, 1956). Good brief accounts of Nebuchadrezzar and his Babylon are to be read in the following articles by O. L. Oppenheim, the first of which lists further, more detailed references: "Assyria and Babylonia," IDB, vol. 1, pp. 262–304, and "Nebuchadnezzar," IDB, vol. 3, p. 529f.

2. A short summary of the place in history of Pharaoh Neco is given in J. W. Wilson, "Neco," IDB, vol. 3, p. 530f.

3. The letter of King Adon of Ashkelon, including a photograph of the papyrus sheet on which it was written, was first published by A. Dupont-Sommer, *Semitica*, 1 (1948), pp. 43–68. However, the translation contained in this volume follows that of H. L. Ginsberg, BASOR, 111 (1948), pp. 24–27. Because of the damaged condition of the letter, any translation involves a certain amount of conjecture, and doubts have been expressed concerning its alleged origin during the Babylonian assault on Ashkelon. For full references, see John Bright, *A History of Israel*, OTL (Philadelphia: Westminster, 1972), p. 326, n. 50.

4. Wiseman, *op. cit.*, p. 71. (Proper names as used in this book have been substituted for the sake of consistency.)

5. *Ibid.*, p. 73.

6. Nebuchadrezzar's building inscription, one of a number of such records found in the ruins of ancient Babylon, is quoted by R. Campbell Thompson in *The Cambridge Ancient History* (Cambridge: The University Press, 1929), vol. 3, p. 217.

7. The prayer of Nebuchadrezzar to Marduk is probably a priestly composition and not that of the king himself. Yet it must surely reflect the attitude of

Nebuchadrezzar for, in spite of a certain nobility of tone, it is largely self-serving. The prayer is quoted by G. S. Goodspeed, *A History of the Babylonians and Assyrians* (London: Smith, Elder, and Co., 1903), p. 348, and is repeated by Jack Finegan, *Light from the Ancient Past* (Princeton: Princeton University Press, 1959), p. 225.

8. The Book of the Law discovered during the renovation of the Temple has been the subject of much debate. Was this an actual discovery of a genuinely lost manuscript, or did Hilkiah, the high priest who showed the scroll to King Josiah, simply bring forward material which either he or someone else had placed in the Temple for safekeeping or had "planted" there for such a disclosure as is related in 2 Kings 22? Also, of what was this Book of the Law composed?

With respect to the first question, no certain answer will ever be known. The opinion that the scroll was placed there by Hilkiah with a view toward its later revelation and the alternative solution, i.e., that it was an unanticipated discovery, can both be claimed with equal reasonableness.

Concerning the content of the material, most scholars feel that it constitutes the core of our present Old Testament Book of Deuteronomy, although efforts to identify that core with precision have not been completely successful. See J. Bright, *op. cit.*, p. 318, and G. von Rad, *Deuteronomy*, translated by Dorothea Barton, OTL (Philadelphia: Westminster, 1966), p. 23f.

9. The history of Israel written during Josiah's reign is commonly referred to by scholars as the Deuteronomic History (but here simply as the "Great History"), because it seems to have been inspired by and enjoys close affinities with the material in the biblical Book of Deuteronomy. The view adopted in this study —that the Deuteronomic History originally concluded with 2 Kings 23:25, and that subsequent portions were added later in light of Josiah's death and in view of the experiences of the exile—is spelled out in some detail by N. H. Snaith, "Introduction and Exegesis of 1 and 2 Kings," IB, vol. 3, p. 10f. See also P. R. Ackroyd, *Exile and Restoration*, OTL (Philadelphia: Westminster, 1968), pp. 62– 83; J. Gray, *I & II Kings* (Revised Edition), OTL (Philadelphia: Westminster, 1963), pp. 6–9; J. A. Scoggin, *Joshua*, translated by R. A. Wilson, OTL (Philadelphia: Westminster, 1972), pp. 3–7; G. E. Wright, "Introduction and Exegesis of Deuteronomy," IB, vol. 2, pp. 323–29.

For more information on the writing of history in Israel generally, see C. R. North, "History," IDB, vol. 2, pp. 607–12. On Deuteronomy and the Deuteronomistic school, see G. von Rad, "Deuteronomy," IDB, vol. 1, pp. 831–38, and J. Muilenberg, "The History of the Religion of Israel," IB, vol. 1, pp. 324–26.

10. A curious puzzle hangs about the head of Jehoiakim, who was to preside over the fortunes of his country for eleven of the most turbulent years of her life. The biblical record indicates that he was two years older than his half brother Jehoahaz, twenty five compared to twenty three years of age. Yet it had been Jehoahaz who had succeeded their father and not Jehoiakim, and the wording of 2 Kings 23:30, which describes the accession of the younger Jehoahaz to the Judean throne, suggests that his choice was the result of popular sentiment. For some unexplained reason the rule of primogeniture was thus laid aside and suspicion cast upon the ability or the loyalty of Jehoiakim. Perhaps he was con-

sidered temperamentally incompetent to rule, and so was passed over in favor of his younger brother. Or he may previously have expressed strong Egyptian sympathies, an inclination which would certainly be in keeping with his later behavior, and was thus rejected by the people as a poor successor to the freedom loving Josiah. Whatever the answers, Jehoiakim was certainly the preferable candidate in the eyes of Neco and, as political power lay with the sword, Jehoahaz was led down in order that the older brother might be Pharaoh's regent over the land.

11. No understanding of the final years of the Kingdom of Judah can be attempted without coming to terms with the contribution made by Jeremiah of Anathoth. Yet every student of this prophet's life and work soon comes upon the hard fact that, although the book which bears his name provides a wealth of biographical material (more than we are given for any other prophetic figure in the Old Testament), much of that material and many of Jeremiah's oracles are undated. Furthermore, the scientific analysis of the Book of Jeremiah discloses a history of editing subsequent to the prophet's lifetime, much of it by scribes of the Deuteronomistic school, so that it is frequently difficult to determine with certainty which are the prophet's own words and which are the editorial overlays. Both of these realities frequently render quite difficult an accurate chronological reconstruction of the prophet's life and a close correlation of the prophet's activity to events in his world.

An indication of this difficulty is seen in the fact that two major and more recent studies of Jeremiah differ with the traditional reconstruction of the prophet's life and with each other in important respects. J. P. Hyatt, "Introduction and Exegesis of Jeremiah," IB, vol. 5, pp. 777–1142, argues that Jeremiah's ministry did not begin in 626 B.C., as commonly supposed, but only with the reign of Jehoiakim in 609 (*op. cit.*, p. 779). Hyatt also considers that, instead of being in sympathy with the ideals of Josiah's Reformation of 621, Jeremiah may actually opposed them (p. 780).

On the other hand, J. Bright, *Jeremiah*, AB 21 (Garden City: Doubleday, 1965), denies the existence of a "silent period" by Jeremiah between the year in which Josiah's Reformation began and that of the king's death, as is usually argued by other scholars. Instead, Bright prefers to view the prophet as active during this entire period and, to that end, attributes to the years in question (621–609) certain of Jeremiah's oracles which are traditionally given an earlier provenance (*op. cit.*, p. xcii f.).

Each student of Jeremiah must, of course, weigh the evidence and decide for himself or herself on such matters. In the absence of compelling reasons to do otherwise, this volume largely accepts the traditional interpretation of Jeremiah's life, including the view of his increasing pessimism toward the end that Judah would repent or be spared the tragedy which awaited her.

In addition to Hyatt and Bright, the interested student should also consult J. Muilenburg, "Jeremiah the Prophet," IDB, vol. 2, pp. 823–35. All of these treatments provide ample further references.

12. J. B. Pritchard, ed., *Ancient Near Eastern Texts Relating to the Old Testament*, (Princeton: Princeton University Press, 1969), p. 308.

13. *Ibid.*, p. 321f.

14. The exile of the Jews to Babylon, carried out in two, or possibly three waves by Nebuchadrezzar, is a most perplexing period in biblical history for the simple reason that, as it is virtually undocumented by contemporary records, its details are largely unknown. (In addition to the deportations of 597 and 587, a third of 581 is suggested by Jeremiah 52:30. There is, however, no other reference to such a third deportation.) Not only do the Hebrew historians fail to record the events or conditions in captivity, but the Babylonian Chronicle, awkwardly breaking off after 594, casts into the shadows the very era of which the scriptural record also leaves us ignorant. We do, of course, possess literature of the exile, chiefly Ezekiel, parts of the Deuteronomic History, Isaiah 40f., and the Priestly History, and from it certain facts may be inferred. The reconstruction of the period contained in this volume is based on such inferences and on the small amounts of evidence which archaeology has yielded, with only a modicum of fiction (as the above account of Zedekiah's entrance into Babylon) introduced to fill the gaps.

Scholarly treatment of conditions and developments during the exile may be found in P. R. Ackroyd, *op. cit.*, and J. A. Sanders, "Exile," IDB, vol. 2, pp. 186–88.

15. The student of Ezekiel must wrestle with the fact that, whereas the oracles of this prophet of the exile are reproduced in graphic detail, the context in which they are delivered is often omitted, and biographical data about the man himself are almost non-existent. In both of these respects, the Old Testament record of the person and work of Ezekiel contrasts sharply with that of Jeremiah. Reflecting this uncertainty is the debate which has raged for many years over whether Ezekiel lived and worked in Babylon, in Jerusalem, or in both. The present treatment has opted for a Babylonian setting for Ezekiel's work, although given the relative ease with which some Jews seem to have moved between Babylon and Jerusalem during the exilic years, serious consideration must be given to the possibility that some of the prophet's experiences, such as those related in Ezekiel 11:1–13 (see p. 76), took place in Jerusalem.

That Ezekiel was born in 622 B.C. and that his life followed the chronology outlined here is based on the assumption, made by many scholars, but doubted by others, that the "thirtieth year" in Ezekiel 1:1 is that of the prophet's life.

As in the case of the Book of Jeremiah, that of Ezekiel has been subjected to a variety of editorial hands over the years. The oracles referred to in this volume are among those which are generally believed to preserve the essence of the prophet's thought.

Good treatments of Ezekiel and the problems raised by the literature which bears his name may be found in W. Eichrodt, *Ezekiel*, translated by Cosslett Quin, OTL (Philadelphia: Westminster, 1970); C. G. Howie, "Ezekiel," IDB, vol. 2, pp. 203–13, and H. G. May, "Interpretation and Exegesis of Ezekiel, IB, vol. 6, pp. 41–337.

16. This description of the life of Amel-Marduk is a reconstruction based on the few "hard" facts about him that have survived: that he was the son of Nebuchadrezzar and that his brief rule was followed by that of his brother-in-law, Nergal-shar-usur. See A. L. Oppenheim, "Evil-Merodach," IDB, vol. 2, p. 183.

17. For a thorough discussion of the Holiness Code see M. Noth, *Leviticus*, translated by J. E. Anderson, OTL (Philadelphia: Westminster, 1965), pp. 127–201.

18. The biographical sketch of Nergal-shar-usur is based upon much more solid evidence than that of his predecessor, Amel-Marduk. The single tablet of the Babylonian Chronicle relating to his reign which has survived portrays a vigorous, commanding, and aggressive figure, and suggests that his domestic affairs were handled with the same efficiency and energy as his military adventures. See D. J. Wiseman, *op. cit.*, pp. 37–42, for a discussion of Nergal-shar-usur, and pp. 75–77 for the text of the tablet which describes his campaign against Appuasu.

19. Wiseman, *op. cit.*, p. 77.

20. The treatment in this volume of the Priestly History, or "P", as it is sometimes known, relies heavily upon the study of P. R. Ackroyd, *op. cit.*, pp. 84–102, and upon G. von Rad, *Genesis*, translated by J. H. Marks, OTL, Revised Ed., (Philadelphia; Westminster, 1972), pp. 47–66. It must be stressed that the precise ending of the Priestly History is a matter of debate. The view adopted here is that the Priestly narrative of the death of Moses, which may be detected in Deuteronomy 32:48–52 and 34:1, 7–9, originally formed the conclusion to the Priestly History and that the catalogue of tribal lands in Joshua 13–19 (or perhaps 13–21), also from "P", initially stood with the similar Priestly material in Numbers 33f., but was transferred to the account of the Conquest by a later editor, perhaps the one responsible for the final form of the Hexateuch. (See especially Ackroyd, p. 97.)

21. For the texts of the Babylonian and Canaanite myths, see Pritchard, *op. cit.*, pp. 60–72, 129–42.

22. Nabonidus, the last of the New Babylonian rulers, has remained a shadowy figure for, in spite of the best efforts of archaeologists and historians to reconstruct the events of his rule, very little solid evidence for such a reconstruction has survived. See A. L. Oppenheim, "Nabonidus," IDB, vol. 3, p. 493f.

23. Pritchard, *op. cit.*, p. 309.

24. *Ibid.*, pp. 311f., 560f.

25. *Ibid.*, p. 306.

26. Concerning Cyrus, the founder of the Persian Empire, there is happily a bit more information than concerning his contemporary Nabonidus. A. T. Olmstead, *History of the Persian Empire* (Chicago: The University of Chicago Press, 1948, 1959), although an older work, is still classic. And H.W.F. Saggs, *The Greatness That Was Babylon* (London: Sidgwick and Jackson, 1962) is of much help in understanding Cyrus and Nabonidus and the relationship between them. Important primary sources, among which are the "Nabonidus Chronicle" and the "Cyrus Cylinder," are reproduced in English in Pritchard, *op. cit.*, pp. 305f., 315f.

27. Pritchard, *op. cit.*, p. 306.

28. The Babylonian Isaiah, or as he is more commonly called in scholarly circles, the Second or Deutero Isaiah, has been the subject of intensive debate since his existence was first postulated by J. G. Eichhorn in 1783. Today, however they may disagree on details, most serious analysts of the material in Isaiah 40–55 agree that it is from the hand of an anonymous prophet of the exile, rather than from that of Isaiah of Jerusalem who lived and worked in the eighth century B.C. (The subsequent chapters in the Book of Isaiah, 56–66, are often attributed to still another prophet of the Isaianic tradition who was active, probably in Jerusalem, shortly after the Judean Restoration.)

The literature on the Babylonian Isaiah is extensive and the following references represent better, more recent treatments which will introduce the reader to the wider questions surrounding this intriguing figure. Good, brief summaries of the reasons for assuming the prophet's existence may be found in J. L. McKenzie, *Second Isaiah*, AB 20 (Garden City: Doubleday, 1968) p. xv f., and C. R. North, "Isaiah," IDB, vol. 2, pp. 731–44 (see especially p. 737f.). The former reference, in addition to being a fine commentary generally, also includes a good history of the scholarly efforts to come to terms with the Second Isaiah and his work. Further helpful aids are C. R. North, *The Second Isaiah* (Oxford: The Clarendon Press, 1964) and C. Westermann, *Isaiah 40–66*, translated by D.G.M. Stalker, OTL (Philadelphia: Westminster, 1969).

The questions surrounding the so-called "Servant Poems" have become a field of inquiry in themselves. A brief overview may be read in C. R. North, "The Servant of the Lord," IDB, vol. 4, p. 292f., while the most extensive treatment in print is the same author's *The Suffering Servant in Deutero-Isaiah* (London: Geoffrey Cumberlege, Oxford University Press, 1956).

29. Pritchard, *op. cit.*, p. 315.

30. The most extended account in the Bible of the Fall of Babylon, that contained in Daniel 5, was written several centuries after the event and is more concerned to recount the exploits of the legendary Daniel than to provide detailed information of a military or political nature. See S. B. Frost, "Daniel," IDB, vol. 1, p. 761f., A. A. Di Lella, "Daniel," IDB, Supplementary Volume, p. 205f., and N. W. Porteus, *Daniel*, OTL (Philadelphia: Westminster, 1965), esp. p. 76f.

31. This story of the Jewish farmer is, of course, an imaginative reconstruction. The entire effort to piece together the details of the Judean Restoration is rendered extremely difficult by the scarcity of pertinent non-biblical materials and by the fact that accounts in the Bible itself are only tangentially concerned with the historical record of the period (Haggai, Zechariah, Chronicles) or treat that history with less than perfect precision (Ezra, Nehemiah). Valuable discussions of the problems surrounding this period in Israel's life may be found in a number of works, especially J. Bright, *A History of Israel*, second edition (Philadelphia: Westminster, 1972), p. 360f., and P. Ackroyd, *op. cit.*, pp. 138–52.

32. The treatment in this volume assumes that Sheshbazzar and Zerubbabel are separate personalities (not, as is sometimes claimed, two names for the same

individual) who were successive governors of Jerusalem and that Sheshbazzar laid the foundations of the Second Temple (Ezra 5:14, but see Zech. 4:9), whereas Zerubbabel completed the edifice. See B. T. Dahlberg, "Sheshbazzar," IDB, vol. 4, p. 325f., and the same author's "Zerubbabel," IDB, vol. 4, p. 955f.

33. See M. J. Dresden, "Darius," IDB, vol. 1, p. 769f.

34. One of these was an individual who professed to be the son of the Babylonian prince Bel-shar-usur and who led the people of that city in a short lived revolt under the title Nebuchadrezzar III.

35. The role of the prophets Haggai and Zechariah in urging the rebuilding of the Temple and in calling for the coronation of Zerubbabel as the Davidic king has been traditionally understood. Instructive discussions of the work of these men and of the books which bear their names may be found in W. Neil, "Haggai," IDB, vol. 2, pp. 509–11, and the same author's "Zechariah, Book of," IDB, vol. 4, pp. 943–947, in D. W. Thomas, "Interpretation and Exegesis of Haggai," IB, vol. 6, pp. 1037–1049, and his "Interpretation and Exegesis of Zechariah," IB, vol. 6, pp. 1053–1088. With most commentators, our presentation assumes that chapters 9–14 of Zechariah reflect the work of someone other than the prophetic contemporary of Haggai.

36. For a discussion of the frequently made proposal that Zechariah 6:11 should read "Zerubbabel" instead of "Joshua," see Ackroyd, op. cit., p. 194f.

37. 1 & 2 Chronicles were for long considered, and are still so considered by many today, as dating from the century after the Judean Restoration. D. N. Freedman, "The Chronicler's Purpose," Catholic Biblical Quarterly, 22 (1961), pp. 436–42, seems to have first published the understanding of the Chronicler's work which places it in the context of the Judean Restoration. Recent contributions on the subject have included F. M. Cross, "A Reconstruction of the Judean Restoration," JBL (94), March 1975, pp. 4–18, and J. D. Newsome, "Toward a New Understanding of the Chronicler and His Purposes," JBL (94), June 1975, pp. 201–17. The latter article contains a brief history of the scholarly interpretation of Chronicles. The best recent commentary on Chronicles is the two volume work of J. M. Myers, I Chronicles, AB 12, and II Chronicles, AB 13. However, Professor Myers subscribes to the view that Chronicles was written about 400 B.C., well after the era of Zerubbabel.

38. The Books of Ezra and Nehemiah present special problems for the interpreter because of their apparent frequent confusion concerning persons and events, perhaps the most discussed of these being the chronological sequence in which the two principals worked in the restored Jerusalem. In spite of strong arguments which have been advanced that the mission of Nehemiah preceeded that of Ezra, the chronology followed here is based upon that outlined by F. M. Cross, op. cit. Further fruitful discussions may be read in R. A. Bowman, "Introduction and Exegesis of Ezra and Nehemiah," IB, vol. 3, pp. 551–68, J. M. Myers, Ezra, Nehemiah, AB 14, and R. H. Pfeiffer, "Ezra and Nehmiah," IDB, vol. 2, pp. 215–19.

39. For those interested in the history of Jerusalem and in that of the city's successive temples, much valuable information will be found in M. Burrows, "Jerusalem," IDB, vol. 2, pp. 843–66, J. Comay, *The Temple of Jerusalem* (London: Widenfeld & Nicholson, 1975), and W. F. Stinespring, "Temple," IDB, vol. 4, pp. 534–60.

40. Rolf Hochhuth, *The Deputy* (New York: Grove Press, 1964), pp. 225–26.